30-Minute Instant Pot Cookbook

30-MINUTE Instant Pot COOKBOOK

Quick and Easy Recipes for Every Meal

RAMONA CRUZ-PETERS

ROCKRIDGE
PRESS

For general information on our other products and services or to obtain technical support, please contact our Customer Care Department within the United States at (866) 744-2665, or outside the United States at (510) 253-0500.

Rockridge Press publishes its books in a variety of electronic and print formats. Some content that appears in print may not be available in electronic books, and vice versa.

TRADEMARKS: Rockridge Press and the Rockridge Press logo are trademarks or registered trademarks of Callisto Media Inc. and/or its affiliates, in the United States and other countries, and may not be used without written permission. All other trademarks are the property of their respective owners. Rockridge Press is not associated with any product or vendor mentioned in this book.

Interior and Cover Designer: Darren Samuel
Art Producer: Hannah Dickerson
Editor: Marjorie DeWitt
Production Editor: Rachel Taenzler
Production Manager: David Zapanta

Photography © 2021 Andrew Purcell, food styling by Carrie Purcell, cover, back cover (center, bottom) and pp. II, VI, VIII, X, 28, 32, 44, 50, 56, 62, 72, 78, 82, 94, 108, 114, 118, 124, 130, 136, 138; © Marija Vidal, back cover (top) and pp. 24, 38, 42; © Hélène Dujardin, pp. 18, 76, 126; © Laura Flippen, pp. 90, 102; © Darren Muir, p. 93.

Front cover: Spicy Broccoli Beef (page 98)
Paperback ISBN: 978-1-63807-676-6
eBook ISBN: 978-1-63878-280-3
R0

This is for the dream chasers
(especially those closest to me: Nik, Grayson, and Sawyer).

Contents

Introduction

The Instant Pot changed the game for me. Rice and vegetables cook quickly and effort-lessly, meats become unbelievably tender, and flavors blend together for the most savory sauces. As someone who lives for quick and easy meal solutions (especially on busy school nights around my kids' activities), one of the Instant Pot's selling points is how quickly food can be prepared. However, I discovered that many pressure cooker recipes can be misleading. A recipe may report a 15-minute cook time, but if that doesn't account for the time it takes for the Instant Pot to reach or release pressure, that 15 minutes can be closer to 45 minutes in reality.

My last book, *Pressure Cooker Cookbook for Beginners*, was all about introducing you to the device and showing you the possibilities; a practical guide along with a variety of recipes. *30-Minute Instant Pot Cookbook* is your everyday go-to for quick meals. You'll find delicious recipes for breakfast, lunch, dinner, dessert, and your favorite pantry staples. The best part? Every recipe in this book can be completely prepped and prepared in 30 minutes or less!

Just like the recipes and projects on my website, Fab Everyday, the recipes in this book are written for real life. The ingredients are easy to shop for, and the dishes are easy to prepare (without sacrificing taste) so they add to, not take away from, your life. Whether you're cooking for a smaller group or for a crowd, the recipes can be scaled easily without affecting the cooking time.

Whatever your amount of cooking experience, you'll be making quick, easy Instant Pot meals in no time (pun intended) with the clear instructions and honest cooking times given in the recipes ahead. The only thing you need to think about is which recipe you'll make tonight.

Chapter 1

Quick and Easy Instant Pot Cooking

Before you dive into the recipes, learn how to use the Instant Pot and what you'll need (and what you'll need to know) to work faster and more efficiently in the kitchen. But don't worry; we'll keep this section quick.

The Ultimate Kitchen Time Saver

Whether you are a busy person with a lot on your plate throughout the week, or someone who likes to keep things simple in the kitchen, you should have a number of tried-and-true 30-minute meals in your repertoire. I define a 30-minute meal as one that can be completely prepped, cooked, and ready to serve in 30 minutes or less. This often means that the recipes have simpler prep, fewer ingredients, and are generally lower maintenance. I've made it a mission to find and develop recipes that meet these requirements and are also super tasty. Over the years I have found the Instant Pot to be ideal for this type of cooking, because food cooks in the airtight pot under high pressure, allowing trapped steam to cook the food quickly at a high temperature. Because steam doesn't escape from the pot during the cooking time, the flavors and juices infuse back into the ingredients, yielding flavorful, moist, and tender results for dishes such as stews, roasts, risotto, soups, vegetables, and more. It also happens in a shorter amount of time than cooking the same dishes on the stovetop or in the oven. Instant Pot cooking is hands-off once the pot is sealed, so you'll have more time for multitasking while it pressure cooks, because you're not tied to the stove.

Don't get me wrong; not all Instant Pot meals are as quick as you might have been led to believe. Many popular Instant Pot recipes, such as stocks, braises, and roasts, can take anywhere from an hour to 90 minutes to prepare. But as I demonstrate with the recipes in this book, the Instant Pot can most definitely be used to make hearty, complete meals in much less time than that. You just need the right recipes. Because you've got your hands on this book, you're off to a great start for making many satisfying meals (and sides, and desserts) in no more than half an hour. To set yourself up for success, read through the rest of this chapter to understand what types of foods and prep steps lead to great 30-minute Instant Pot meals.

5 Fast Favorites

All the recipes in this book promise to deliver a scrumptious meal (or side, or dessert) in under 30 minutes, but there are a handful that stand out in my mind in terms of both convenience and overall wonderful taste. You'll want to bookmark these, as they will become your new go-to recipes.

1. Sun-Dried Tomato, Spinach, and Feta Egg Bites (page 29): Reminiscent of Starbucks's sous-vide egg bites, these delectable breakfast bites are made easily in a silicone egg mold. They are great for meal prepping, because you can make up to 14 at a time and store them in the refrigerator for a few days.

2. Easy Wonton Soup (page 53): This soup is a family favorite that is on regular rotation in our home. The name says it all: It is surprisingly easy for being so flavorful and filling.

3. Truffled Mushroom Risotto (page 64): If I had to pick one dish alone that made the purchase of an Instant Pot worthwhile, it would be this risotto. Pressure cooking risotto is an absolute game changer. No more standing over the stove, stirring constantly for 30 minutes; Instant Pot risotto is hands-off and perfect every time.

4. Cheeseburger Macaroni (page 101): This homemade version of cheeseburger mac is just as easy as the boxed stuff, but more than twice as good.

5. Mini Funfetti Cupcakes (page 116): Many people are surprised to learn that you can make fluffy "baked goods" in a pressure cooker. Because they are technically steamed in a high-pressure environment (not baked), the results are moist and full of flavor. These mini cupcakes are one of my kids' favorite Instant Pot recipes.

Keys to Quick Cooking with the Instant Pot

As I mentioned earlier in this chapter, certain foods take longer to cook in the Instant Pot. That being said, there are also foods that cook more quickly than others. Knowing the foods, prep steps, and techniques that can reduce overall cooking time is key to quick Instant Pot meals.

Let someone else prep. Many grocery stores offer fresh, cut or sliced ingredients, such as beef, chicken, mushrooms, onions, and other vegetables. Although they can cost a few cents more, the time-saving benefits for recipe prep are well worth the cost. Several recipes in this book call for presliced or prechopped ingredients to keep prep time quick and efficient.

Canned convenience. Canned beans and peeled, diced tomatoes are examples of canned foods that both prep and cook considerably faster without any sacrifice of the meal's quality. Yes, the Instant Pot is great for cooking dried beans, but if fast is what you're going for, canned beans are an ideal choice.

Size matters. Under pressure, dense foods take longer to cook than lighter foods. Cutting or slicing thick pieces of meat or vegetables into smaller pieces allows a more even flow of heat and moisture throughout the pot, ensuring a faster cooking time.

Multitask. Because Instant Pot cooking is hands-off at different points, prepping any remaining ingredients while food is simmering or pressure cooking can shave minutes off the overall recipe time. Be sure to read through the recipe first so you know which ingredients should be prepped at the beginning and which can wait to be prepped during later, hands-off cooking steps.

Leverage built-in seasonings. Simple premade sauces and marinades can add a lot of flavor to your meals with fewer ingredients (and therefore less prep). Look for seasoned sauces that can do some of the work for you. Marinade sauces, depending on the flavor, can replace some of the meal's added liquid, salt, vinegar, sugars, and herbs.

Preheat for efficient sautéing. Food will cook faster when added to a pot that's preheated and ready to go. If a recipe includes a sauté step, preheat the pot by selecting the Sauté function while you're prepping the ingredients, so it will be ready to start cooking as soon as your ingredients are ready to be added.

Temperature check. One of the main variables in how long the Instant Pot takes to reach pressure is the temperature of the ingredients (especially liquid ingredients) in the pot. Unless otherwise noted in the recipe, use room-temperature liquids, which will boil (and therefore reach the required pressure point) faster than cold ingredients.

Getting to Know the Pot

For those who don't have a lot of experience with pressure cooking, there is a slight learning curve with the Instant Pot when it comes to understanding the various parts, functions, and terminology, but after reading about the basics and cooking the 30-minute recipes in this book, these functions and terms will become second nature.

Parts

The Instant Pot has parts that may differ from many appliances you're used to, so here's a rundown of the major parts.

Control panel. This panel provides the pot's digital display and programmable buttons.

Inner pot. This is the removable stainless-steel pot that contains the food to be cooked.

Exterior pot. This metal pot is attached to the cooker housing; the inner pot is placed inside the exterior pot. *The exterior pot should not be cooked in directly.*

Heating element. At the bottom of the exterior pot is the heating element, which is much like a stove burner and will heat the inner pot to sauté and bring the pot to pressure.

Lid. The lid locks safely into place before bringing the pot to pressure and houses the steam release mechanism, float valve, and sealing ring.

Steam release. Sometimes called a "pressure release button," this switch, which feels loose (that's normal), can be turned to seal (for pressure to build) or vent (to release the steam and pressure).

Float valve. Sometimes called a "pin," this small metal float valve is the visual indicator of whether there is pressure in the pot or not. When the pin is all the way up, the pot is at full pressure. The pin will drop completely when the pressure is released and to indicate that the pot is safe to open.

Sealing ring. The silicone or rubber sealing ring (sometimes called a "gasket") located on the underside of the lid enables the pot to become airtight. A damaged or improperly placed sealing ring will affect the pot's ability to maintain pressure.

Controls

The digital control panel displays the cook time and messages, such as if the pot is hot and ready to sauté, or if burning is detected. The display also includes the programmable buttons that allow you to choose cook settings and start or stop cooking modes. Here are the main functions that are used to make the recipes in this book.

Pressure Cook. This is the button that will be used most for the recipes in this book. After pressing Pressure Cook, use the [+] and [-] buttons to adjust the cooking time. The countdown will begin after the pot has reached pressure.

Pressure Level. If a recipe indicates a cook time at Low pressure, select Pressure Level after selecting the Pressure Cook time, then adjust the Pressure Level to Low. (The default is High.)

Steam. This is a preprogrammed option that regulates the pressure to maintain a steamy environment with the liquid in the bottom of the pot.

Sauté. The Sauté button will make the inner pot work as any pot would sauté on a stovetop.

Cancel. As the name implies, this will end any Instant Pot cooking or warming function. After sautéing, press Cancel before starting other cooking steps. You can also press Cancel to end the default Keep Warm option after pressure cooking and turn off the pot completely.

A Step-by-Step Guide to Using Your Instant Pot

The following includes examples and explanations of some of the common recipe steps in this cookbook.

Step 1: For recipes that include a sauté step, start by selecting the Sauté button and allow the pot to preheat before adding oil or butter to the pot. When the oil is hot or the butter is melted, you can sauté or sear ingredients in the inner pot much as you would with a pan on a stove. Press Cancel to end the Sauté function before moving on. Before pressure cooking, you should always deglaze the pot by adding a liquid ingredient and scraping the bottom of the pot with a wooden or plastic spoon to loosen any brown bits. This step will also help prevent the Burn error, which is a safety function that will stop the cooking process when it senses the bottom of the inner pot may be too hot (and burn the food).

Step 2: After adding liquid and any other required ingredients (remember that liquid is required for the pot to generate steam and build pressure), close and lock the lid in place. Make sure the Steam Release switch is set to Sealing, and then push the Pressure Cook button (labeled as Manual on some models), and adjust the cooking time according to the recipe. The cooking time will begin automatically when the pot has reached pressure, and a timer will begin counting down.

Step 3: When the cook time ends, the Instant Pot will beep and turn off the heat. Before opening the pot, pressure will need to be released. If the recipe calls for "quick release," use an oven mitt or a wooden spoon to move the Steam Release switch to Venting. (Moving the switch will release hot steam from inside the cooker and could burn your hand.) Make sure to release the steam away from your face or anything you wouldn't want damaged by hot steam. If the recipe calls for "natural release," leave the switch on Sealing while you watch the timer on the pot (which will start counting up after the pressure cooking time ends). Leave the lid on the pot for the stated amount of time, and then follow the steps listed previously to quick release the remaining pressure. With either release method, the pressure must be released completely (when you see and hear the pin drop) before you can unlock and remove the lid.

Once the pot is cool enough to handle, unplug it and clean it entirely (including the valves and gaskets) after each use. If parts become clogged, a safety mechanism may not be able to regulate pressure or create warnings, and your food may not cook properly.

Adjusting Recipes for High-Altitude Cooking

Water evaporates faster at higher altitudes, so if you live anywhere that is 2,000 feet or more above sea level, you will need to adjust the cooking times. As a general rule, recipe cooking times can be adjusted by 5 percent for every 1,000 feet above 2,000 feet (rounding up to the next minute). For example, if you are 3,000 feet above sea level when making Peaches and Cream Oatmeal (page 20), increase the pressure-cooking time from 6 to 7 minutes. The Creamy Broccoli Cheddar Soup (page 46) pressure-cooking time would increase from 2 to 3 minutes.

Note that some Instant Pot models, such as the Ultra and Max, include altitude adjustment features.

Equipment Essentials

These are the tools that get the most use in my kitchen and will be helpful to you as you create the recipes in this cookbook.

Steamer basket with dividers. This basket is useful for smaller vegetables and foods that would otherwise fall between the slats of the trivet that comes with the pot.

7-cup heat-safe bowl (such as a glass Pyrex bowl). This size fits perfectly inside 6- or 8-quart Instant Pots for making pot-in-pot recipes. "Pot-in-pot" (sometimes abbreviated "PIP") is a method where a smaller pot or bowl is placed inside the inner pot. This is a gentler cooking method and is common for recipes where you can't cook the food directly in liquid, or for ingredients that would burn if placed on the bottom of the pot.

Silicone egg bite mold. Not just for eggs, you can also make desserts and other recipes with individual-size portions (such as Mini Funfetti Cupcakes, page 116).

7-inch springform pan. In addition to being perfect for the famous Instant Pot cheesecake, these pans are great for lasagna and other pot-in-pot recipes.

Wooden spoon and silicone-tipped tongs. These tools will help you sauté and move food without scratching the inside of the pot.

Oven mitts. The smaller pinch mitts are helpful for pulling hot trivets out of the pot, or when lifting the still-hot inner pot to clean it.

Extra sealing rings. The sealing ring from the Instant Pot lid absorbs odors, so I recommend having extra rings to designate different ones for savory and sweet recipes.

Stocking the 30-Minute Kitchen

Before cooking the quick and easy recipes in this book, there are some ingredients that you will want to have handy. For the ingredients you don't have already and need to purchase, don't worry; you will get a lot of use out of them, and they will quickly pay for themselves.

Refrigerator Staples

Some common, store-bought fresh ingredients will serve as the backbone of many of the recipes in this book. Here's what I recommend having on hand in your refrigerator.

Chopped onion and sliced mushrooms. Prechopped onion and presliced mushrooms from the grocery store shave minutes off recipe prep.

Cream cheese. One of the ways to make Instant Pot pastas creamier is by using cream cheese rather than another dairy product.

Eggs. Whether you hardboil eggs or use them in breakfast casseroles, Instant Pots cook eggs to perfection.

Heavy (whipping) cream. Because milk tends not to cook well under pressure (and is prone to curdling), the higher fat content of heavy cream makes it a better choice for rich, creamy sauces.

Minced garlic. For super quick prep, jarred minced garlic is a great replacement for fresh minced garlic. Use ½ teaspoon of jarred minced garlic in place of each garlic clove.

Plain, unsweetened yogurt. Yogurt is a secret ingredient for making Instant Pot "baked goods" light and fluffy.

Real unsalted butter. Although margarine can sometimes substitute for butter, sweet breakfasts and desserts will always come out better when you use real unsalted butter.

Soy sauce or tamari. These rich and salty sauces are necessary for many Asian-style recipes and are high-impact additions to non-Asian-style meat marinades.

Pantry Staples

The recipes in this book lean heavily on a small number of pantry items (a mix of ingredients you likely have and a few you will probably need to acquire). Here are some that I always have in my pantry.

Cajun seasoning. A good all-purpose Cajun seasoning adds flavor and spice to recipes.

Chicken stock. Stock adds savoriness to sauces, rice, and steamed dishes.

Cornstarch. Because sauces don't reduce while pressure cooking, adding a mixture of cornstarch and water after pressure cooking is a great way to thicken them.

Flour, sugar, and brown sugar. I find light brown sugar to be more versatile than dark brown sugar if you only have space for one type.

Garlic. Keep a fresh head of garlic at room temperature to grab cloves as needed.

Garlic powder and onion powder. I use garlic powder in almost every savory recipe, and onion powder can really take a sauce to the next level.

Ginger. I keep ground ginger in my spice cabinet and fresh ginger in my freezer (it lasts longer in the freezer and small amounts can be grated or sliced as needed).

Oats. Old-fashioned oats are excellent for oatmeal and crumble toppings.

Salt and pepper. I recommend stocking table salt, coarse salt, and peppercorns for freshly ground black pepper.

Vegetable oil, olive oil, and sesame oil. I always have these three oils stocked. Sesame oil is a secret ingredient for most of my Asian-inspired recipes.

5 Tips for Smart Shopping

Smart shopping is a great way to save time. Keep these shopping tips in mind to keep your meal planning and cooking processes easier and more affordable.

1. Double-up. For foods that come in larger packs (such as chicken thighs, sliced mushrooms, and rice), plan to shop for multiple recipes that use these core ingredients. This is not only efficient for shopping, it also reduces food waste.

2. Look for what's in season. Fruits and vegetables that are in season are also often on sale because stores have them in abundance at those times of year.

3. Organize your list. Rather than rewriting my grocery shopping list, I add a code to the beginning of each item on the list based on the grocery store aisle ("P" for produce, "D" for dairy, "M" for meat, and so on). This makes shopping trips quicker and more efficient.

4. Precut ingredients. Many supermarkets have affordable containers of precut vegetables such as carrots, Brussels sprouts, and celery that make meal prep even easier. Also look for these items in the frozen foods section, where they are often available at an even lower price.

5. Shop store brand. Many store brand and generic products are just as good as name brand items, but come with a much lower price tag.

Troubleshooting

Although the Instant Pot is typically a safe and reliable device, it's not totally foolproof. Similar to cooking with any other appliance, mistakes can happen. Here are a few common issues and tips on how to troubleshoot to resolve them.

Burn error. There are a few ways to prevent and fix this frustrating issue. To prevent it, always deglaze the inner pot after sautéing by adding a liquid ingredient and scraping the bottom of the pot with a wooden or plastic spoon to loosen any brown bits. You should also make sure you have enough of a thin liquid in your recipes (1 cup or more for 6-quart pots; 1½ cups or more for 8-quart pots) and avoid thick sugary sauces (e.g., tomato sauce). If you do receive the Burn error, don't fret: Your meal is not necessarily wasted. If the error occurs after the pot has reached pressure, simply leave the food in the pot for the remainder of the cooking time. The Instant Pot will turn off the heat automatically, so there is no danger, and the food will continue to cook in the pot's residual steam.

Food is taking a long time to reach pressure. One of the main variables in how long the Instant Pot takes to reach pressure is the temperature of the ingredients (especially the liquid ingredients) in the pot. Unless otherwise noted in the recipe, use room-temperature liquids that will boil faster (and therefore reach the required pressure point faster) than cold ingredients. If your pot doesn't reach pressure at all, or you see steam escaping from the side of the lid, the most likely cause is an issue with the sealing ring. It is either damaged, or it wasn't replaced on the lid after cleaning.

Food is undercooked. Different Instant Pot models can have cook time variance depending on their size, heat and pressure levels, and sensitivity to heat for the Burn error. You will learn about your own model after using it for a while and may find that your device consistently requires more or less cooking time than a recipe states. If you find that rice

More Ways to Save Time in the Kitchen

Although the recipes in this book can all be made in under 30 minutes, I have some tried-and-true tips and tricks to make prep, cooking, and cleanup even faster.

Meal planning. My number-one tip for efficient cooking is meal planning. It helps you shop for exactly what you need and eliminates the daily what-to-cook-for-dinner debate.

Read the recipe completely before cooking. This helps you know what to prep, and when. Some ingredients can be prepped during passive cooking time to shave minutes off the entire recipe.

Wash produce after buying it. To save yourself a step during recipe prep, wash all your vegetables after a grocery trip before putting them away.

Skip the peeling step. Did you know that most veggies don't require peeling before cooking and eating them? Save yourself time and skip this step.

Quick cutting. Use kitchen shears for super quick cutting of herbs, smaller vegetables, and thinner cuts of meat (e.g., bacon).

Invest in a good knife. You'd be surprised how much time you can save by using a good, sharp chef's knife.

Clean as you go. Clean your prep station during passive cooking time to make cleanup quicker later. You can also plate side dishes and set the table while waiting for the pressure-cooked entrée to finish.

or legumes aren't soft enough after cooking, add ¼ cup more liquid (if completely evaporated), close the lid, and pressure cook for 3 more minutes.

Sauce is too thin. Because sauces don't reduce while pressure cooking, they tend to be thin immediately after cooking. There are a few ways to thicken a sauce. One way is to allow the sauce to reduce while simmering on Sauté mode. Or you can add a cornstarch slurry: Remove 1 tablespoon of liquid from the pot, whisk it with 1 tablespoon of cornstarch in a small bowl, and return it to the pot to sauté for a few minutes. You can use more or less cornstarch depending on your desired thickness.

The Recipes in This Book

The recipes in this book were designed to be easy enough to cook on a busy weeknight using a 6-quart or larger Instant Pot. Most of the recipes serve four to six people, although some breakfasts, sides, and desserts serve two and can be cooked in an Instant Pot Mini. One of the great things about the Instant Pot is how easy it is to scale recipes up or down without much impact (if any) to the cooking time.

All recipes have been tested to ensure that the total cook time—including ingredient prep, active cooking time, time for the unit to reach pressure, and pressure release time—is under 30 minutes. By following the Keys to Quick Cooking with the Instant Pot tips (page 4), you will speed up your prep time and gain efficiencies.

To help with meal planning, some of the recipes include convenience labels indicating whether they are complete one-pot meals (where the main dish and vegetables or sides all cook together in one pot), can be made in under 20 minutes ("Super Quick"—perfect for busy nights), or can be made with five or fewer ingredients (minus the "freebies" of salt, pepper, water, and oil/cooking spray).

As with any recipe, feel free to use the seasoning and spice measurements as a starting point, and adjust them to your taste. Making the recipes your own—by taking advantage of some of the variation, substitution, and flavor-boosting tips included in this cookbook—will give you so much more than the 70 recipes included. My hope is that this book will sit right beside your Instant Pot as another trusted tool in your cooking arsenal.

Nutty Maple Polenta

Page 21

Chapter 2

Breakfast & Brunch

PEACHES AND CREAM OATMEAL

> SERVES 2

> **Prep time:** 3 minutes

> **Pressure cook:** 6 minutes High

> **Release:** Natural for 10 minutes, then Quick Release

> **Total time:** 30 minutes

Once I started making oatmeal in the Instant Pot, I have never made it any other way. I make it as a pot-in-pot recipe, a gentler cooking method that prevents the dreaded Burn warning. You can customize the recipe with your favorite oatmeal add-ins and increase or decrease cooking time depending on how soft or firm you like your oats.

2 cups water, divided

1 cup old-fashioned oats

½ cup milk

2 tablespoons brown sugar

¼ teaspoon vanilla extract

¼ teaspoon ground cinnamon

Pinch salt

1 (15-ounce) can peaches, drained and diced

¼ cup heavy (whipping) cream

1. Pour 1 cup of water into the inner pot and place a steamer rack trivet in the bottom.

2. In a heat-safe bowl, stir together the oats, remaining 1 cup of water, the milk, brown sugar, vanilla, cinnamon, and salt. Place the bowl on the trivet.

3. Close the lid and set the cooking time to 6 minutes at high/normal pressure. It will take 7 to 8 minutes to reach pressure.

4. Allow the pressure to release from the pot naturally for 10 minutes, then quick release the remaining pressure.

5. Remove the bowl from the pot and stir in the peaches and cream. The oatmeal will thicken as it cools.

6. Store leftovers in an airtight container in the refrigerator.

Variation Tip

For a lighter alternative, you can substitute half-and-half, more milk, or your favorite plant-based milk substitute for the heavy cream.

Per serving: Calories: 404; Fat: 16g; Protein: 12g; Carbohydrates: 55g; Fiber: 7g; Sugar: 22g; Sodium: 119mg

NUTTY MAPLE POLENTA

> SERVES 4
> **Prep time:** 2 minutes
> **Sauté:** 5 minutes
> **Pressure cook:** 10 minutes High

> **Release:** Quick
> **Total time:** 25 minutes
> 5-Ingredient

This yummy plant-based breakfast is made from coarsely ground cornmeal. For another way of serving polenta, pour the cooked dish into a loaf pan and let it set for a few hours until firm before cutting it. Reheat slices in the microwave for 30 to 60 seconds and top with more maple syrup and a handful of your favorite berries.

3 cups water

2 cups unsweetened
   plant-based milk

1 cup polenta

½ cup pecan or
   walnut pieces

¼ cup maple syrup

1. Select the Sauté function and whisk together the water, milk, and polenta in the inner pot. Whisk frequently for 5 minutes, until the mixture reaches a simmer, then press Cancel.

2. Close the lid and set the cooking time to 10 minutes at high/normal pressure. It will take 8 minutes to reach pressure.

3. Quick release the pressure. Open the lid and add the nuts and maple syrup and stir well to combine. Serve immediately.

4. Store in a covered container in the refrigerator. The polenta will thicken in the refrigerator but will loosen up when you reheat it in the microwave or on the stovetop over medium heat.

Variation Tip

Turn this into a savory breakfast by omitting the maple syrup and nuts and adding sautéed fresh veggies such as mushrooms, zucchini, spinach, chard, or kale. Top with fresh tomatoes or salsa and sprinkle with a bit of parmesan cheese.

Per serving: Calories: 319; Fat: 12g; Protein: 9g; Carbohydrates: 45g; Fiber: 4g; Sugar: 15g; Sodium: 327mg

SHRIMP AND GRITS

› SERVES 4
› **Prep time:** 2 minutes
› **Pressure cook:** 15 minutes High

› **Release:** Natural for 5 minutes, then Quick Release
› **Total time:** 30 minutes
› One-Pot Meal

One of my favorite Southern breakfasts is shrimp and grits. I order it every time we visit New Orleans. The Instant Pot makes it easy to have this meal any day of the week, not just for vacations or special occasions.

1 cup water	½ teaspoon Cajun seasoning	1 cup shredded cheddar cheese	¼ cup chopped scallions, green parts only
2 cups chicken stock	12 ounces cooked peeled, deveined medium shrimp	⅓ cup real bacon bits	2 tablespoons unsalted butter
1½ cups milk			
1 cup quick grits (not instant grits)			

1. Pour the water into the inner pot and place a steamer rack trivet in the bottom.

2. In a heat-safe bowl, stir together the stock, milk, grits, and Cajun seasoning. Place the bowl on the trivet.

3. Close the lid and set the cooking time to 15 minutes at high/normal pressure. It will take 7 to 8 minutes to reach pressure.

4. Allow the pressure to release from the pot naturally for 5 minutes, then quick release the remaining pressure.

5. Remove the bowl from the pot and stir the shrimp, cheese, bacon, scallions, and butter into the grits. The grits will thicken as it cools.

6. Store leftovers in an airtight container in the refrigerator.

Ingredient Tip

You can also use uncooked shrimp. Stir the shrimp into the grits per the recipe, then return the bowl to the Instant Pot with the lid closed for the shrimp to steam in the hot grits for a few minutes.

Per serving: Calories: 475; Fat: 22g; Protein: 33g; Carbohydrates: 35g; Fiber: 2g; Sugar: 5g; Sodium: 914mg

AVOCADO TOAST WITH POACHED EGG

> SERVES 4
> **Prep time:** 5 minutes
> **Steam:** 3 minutes
> **Release:** Quick

> **Total time:** 15 minutes
> 5-Ingredient, Super Quick

Silicone egg molds and the Instant Pot are game changers for making perfectly poached eggs. You can use this method for making eggs Benedict if you're not in the mood for avocado toast.

| 1 cup water | 4 large eggs | Olive oil, for drizzling | Salt |
| Nonstick cooking spray | 4 slices sourdough bread | 2 avocados, chopped | Freshly ground black pepper |

1. Pour the water into the inner pot and place a steamer rack trivet in the bottom.

2. Spray the cups of a silicone egg mold with cooking spray. Crack an egg into four of the cups, being careful not to break the yolks. Place the egg mold on the trivet.

3. Close the lid and set the cooking time to 3 minutes at steam/normal. It will take 6 minutes to reach pressure.

4. While the eggs are cooking, toast the bread. Drizzle with olive oil and distribute the avocado on top of the toast slices. Smash the avocado lightly with a fork.

5. After the steam time ends, quick release the pressure. Remove the egg mold from the pot. Remove each egg from the mold by running a large spoon between the egg and the cup. Place one egg on top of each piece of avocado toast. Season with salt and pepper and serve immediately.

Flavor Boost

If you want to take this avocado toast to the next level, crumble some goat cheese and sprinkle red pepper flakes on the avocado.

Per serving: Calories: 416; Fat: 22g; Protein: 15g; Carbohydrates: 42g; Fiber: 8g; Sugar: 4g; Sodium: 502mg

EGGS EN COCOTTE

> SERVES 2
> **Prep time:** 5 minutes
> **Sauté:** 14 minutes

> **Pressure cook:** 2 minutes High
> **Release:** Quick
> **Total time:** 30 minutes

Eggs en cocotte is just a fancy term for eggs steamed in cups. They are often flavored with herbs and topped with cheese or cream. This recipe was adapted from *The Art of Living According to Joe Beef: A Cookbook of Sorts.* Serve with the toast of your choosing.

1 tablespoon unsalted butter

1 teaspoon olive oil

4 white button or cremini mushrooms, halved and sliced

1 tablespoon chopped onion

½ cup vegetable stock

½ cup heavy (whipping) cream

1 tablespoon dry sherry

½ teaspoon kosher salt

Pinch freshly ground black pepper

2 large eggs

2 tablespoons grated sharp cheddar cheese

1 cup water

1 tablespoon chopped fresh chives

1. Select the Sauté function and adjust to medium heat. Put the butter and olive oil in the inner pot and heat until the butter is foaming. Add the mushrooms and cook, stirring occasionally, for 5 minutes. Add the onion and cook for 4 minutes or until soft.

2. Add the stock, cream, and sherry and cook for 5 more minutes. Stir in the salt and pepper. Press Cancel.

3. Divide the mixture between two ramekins. Break an egg into each ramekin and sprinkle each with 1 tablespoon of cheddar cheese.

4. Rinse out the pot. Pour the water into the pot and place a steamer rack trivet in the bottom. Place the ramekins, uncovered, on the trivet.

5. Close the lid and set the cooking time to 2 minutes at high/normal pressure (for runny yolks). It will take 7 to 8 minutes to reach pressure.

6. Quick release the pressure. Remove the egg cups and allow to cool for 1 minute before serving garnished with chives.

CONTINUED →

7. If making for meal prep, cover the ramekins with aluminum foil and store in the refrigerator.

Ingredient Tip

To save time, you can buy sliced fresh mushrooms at most markets; just remember that they won't last as long in the refrigerator as whole mushrooms.

Per serving: Calories: 393; Fat: 38g; Protein: 10g; Carbohydrates: 5g; Fiber: 1g; Sugar: 3g; Sodium: 348 mg

PULLED PORK HASH

› SERVES 4
› **Prep time:** 5 minutes
› **Pressure cook:** 2 minutes High
› **Sauté:** 9 minutes

› **Release:** Quick
› **Total time:** 25 minutes
› One-Pot Meal

This breakfast hash is a great way to use leftover pulled pork. We like our breakfast potatoes to be a little firm, but you can add one more minute of pressure-cooking time if you prefer softer potatoes. If desired, serve topped with a fried egg.

1 cup water
2 large potatoes, cut into ½-inch cubes
1 tablespoon unsalted butter

1 tablespoon olive oil
½ cup chopped onion
¼ teaspoon seasoning salt

¼ teaspoon garlic salt
¼ teaspoon freshly ground black pepper
⅛ teaspoon cayenne pepper

1 cup leftover or prepared pulled pork
¼ cup barbecue sauce

1. Pour the water into the inner pot and place a steamer rack trivet in the bottom.

2. Arrange the potatoes in a steamer basket. Place the basket on the trivet.

3. Close the lid and set the cooking time to 2 minutes at high/normal pressure. It will take 7 minutes to reach pressure.

4. Quick release the pressure. Remove the basket and trivet and discard the water.

5. Select the Sauté function and heat the butter and oil in the pot. Add the onion and sauté for 1 to 2 minutes until slightly softened. Add the cooked potatoes, seasoning salt, garlic salt, black pepper, and cayenne to the pot and toss together. Sauté, stirring occasionally, for 5 to 6 minutes or until the edges of the potatoes start to crisp.

6. Stir in the pork and barbecue sauce and sauté, stirring often, for 1 more minute. Press Cancel. Store leftovers in an airtight container in the refrigerator.

Flavor Boost

Add shredded cheddar cheese and chopped chives to make this pulled pork hash "fully loaded."

Per serving: Calories: 290; Fat: 8g; Protein: 13g; Carbohydrates: 42g; Fiber: 5g; Sugar: 8g; Sodium: 209mg

SUN-DRIED TOMATO, SPINACH, AND FETA EGG BITES

> SERVES 7
> **Prep time:** 5 minutes
> **Pressure cook:** 11 minutes High

> **Release:** Natural for 5 minutes, then Quick Release
> **Total time:** 30 minutes
> One-Pot Meal

These scrumptious breakfast bites are reminiscent of Starbucks's sous-vide egg bites. They are great for meal prepping, because you can make up to 14 at a time and store them in the refrigerator for a few days.

1 cup water
Nonstick cooking spray
4 large eggs

½ cup crumbled feta cheese
¼ cup cottage cheese
¼ cup diced sun-dried tomatoes

¼ cup finely chopped spinach
¼ teaspoon freshly ground black pepper

¼ teaspoon garlic powder
⅛ teaspoon salt

1. Pour the water into the inner pot and place a steamer rack trivet in the bottom.

2. Spray the cups of a silicone egg bite mold with cooking spray. In a medium bowl, whisk the eggs. Stir in the feta, cottage cheese, sun-dried tomatoes, spinach, pepper, garlic powder, and salt.

3. Divide the mixture evenly among seven egg bite mold cups. Place the egg bite mold on the trivet.

4. Close the lid and set the cooking time to 11 minutes at high/normal pressure. It will take 6 minutes to reach pressure.

5. Allow the pressure to release from the pot naturally for 5 minutes, then quick release the remaining pressure. Use a butter knife to remove the bites from the mold. Serve.

Variation Tip

Some of my favorite egg bite combinations are ham and cheddar, and bacon and Gruyere.

Per serving: Calories: 82; Fat: 5g; Protein: 6g; Carbohydrates: 2g; Fiber: 0g; Sugar: 1g; Sodium: 216mg

FRENCH TOAST CUPS

> SERVES 4
> **Prep time:** 8 minutes
> **Steam:** 8 minutes High

> **Release:** Natural for 5 minutes, then Quick Release
> **Total time:** 30 minutes

It might seem odd to use an Instant Pot for French toast, but not only is the French toast delicious, this method is much less messy than making it the traditional way. It also yields perfectly uniform servings without having to time how long the bread soaks in the egg mixture.

1 cup water	1 cup whole milk	¼ teaspoon vanilla extract	Pinch salt
3 tablespoons unsalted butter, divided	¼ cup heavy (whipping) cream	1 teaspoon orange juice concentrate	4 cups (¾-inch) bread cubes (4 or 5 bread slices)
2 large eggs			

1. Pour the water into the inner pot and place a steamer rack trivet in the bottom.

2. Using about 1 tablespoon of butter, coat the bottoms and sides of 4 small (1- to 1½-cup) ramekins or custard cups.

3. In a large bowl, whisk the eggs until the yolks and whites are completely mixed. Add the milk, cream, vanilla, orange juice concentrate, and salt and whisk to combine. Add the bread cubes and gently stir to coat with the egg mixture. Let sit for 2 to 3 minutes to let the bread absorb some of the custard, then gently stir again. Spoon the mixture evenly into the prepared cups. Cover each cup with aluminum foil.

4. Place the ramekins on the trivet, stacking if necessary.

5. Close the lid and set the cooking time to 8 minutes at steam/normal. It will take 7 to 8 minutes to reach pressure.

6. Allow the pressure to release from the pot naturally for 5 minutes, then quick release the remaining pressure.

7. Remove the ramekins from the pot. Remove the foil and let cool for a few minutes. Meanwhile, melt the remaining 2 tablespoons of butter in a large skillet or griddle over medium heat. Unmold the French toasts. When the butter has just stopped foaming, place the French toasts in the skillet and cook for about 2 minutes or until golden brown. Turn and brown the other side, 1 to 2 minutes more. Serve immediately.

Variation Tip

To prepare these as a make-ahead breakfast, follow the recipe, then refrigerate the cups after cooling. To serve, heat them for a minute in a microwave, then sauté in butter to crisp up and finish heating through.

Per serving: Calories: 195; Fat: 15g; Protein: 6g; Carbohydrates: 9g; Fiber: 1g; Sugar: 6g; Sodium: 239mg

Broccoli with Creamy
Lemon Sauce

Page 34

Chapter 3

Vegetables & Sides

BROCCOLI WITH CREAMY LEMON SAUCE

› SERVES 4

› **Prep time:** 5 minutes

› **Pressure cook:** 0 minutes High

› **Sauté:** 5 minutes

› **Release:** Quick

› **Total time:** 20 minutes

› 5-Ingredient, Super Quick

One of my favorite reasons for owning an Instant Pot is how quickly it cooks vegetables. I love how broccoli comes out perfectly crisp-tender. This recipe makes an easy, creamy sauce, sautéed using your Instant Pot as a double boiler.

2 cups water, divided	¼ cup light mayonnaise	2 tablespoons milk	2 tablespoons freshly squeezed lemon juice
3 cups broccoli florets	¼ cup sour cream		

1. Pour 1 cup of water into the inner pot and place a steamer rack trivet in the bottom.

2. Arrange the broccoli in a steamer basket. Place the basket on the trivet.

3. Close the lid and set the cooking time to 0 minutes at high/normal pressure. It will take 6 minutes to reach pressure.

4. Quick release the pressure. Remove the basket and trivet from the pot and set aside.

5. Pour the remaining 1 cup of water into the pot and place the steamer rack trivet in the bottom. Select the Sauté function and bring the water to a simmer.

6. In a heat-safe glass or stainless-steel bowl, stir together the mayonnaise, sour cream, milk, and lemon juice. Place the bowl on the trivet.

7. Cook over the simmering water for 5 minutes or until heated through, stirring constantly.

8. Pour the mayonnaise mixture over the broccoli and serve immediately.

Variation Tip

Make this recipe with green beans instead of broccoli, using the same directions and cooking time.

Per serving: Calories: 110; Fat: 9g; Protein: 3g; Carbohydrates: 6g; Fiber: 2g; Sugar: 2g; Sodium: 149mg

HONEY-GARLIC CARROTS

› SERVES 4
› **Prep time:** 5 minutes
› **Pressure cook:** 2 minutes High
› **Sauté:** 6 minutes

› **Release:** Quick
› **Total time:** 20 minutes
› 5-Ingredient, Super Quick

If you're in a rut with your vegetable side dishes, these sweet and savory carrots are just what the doctor ordered. Prepped and cooked in 20 minutes, these carrots will become one of your go-to dinner side dishes. Using mini cut carrots saves time on prep.

1 cup water
1 (16-ounce) pack mini cut carrots

3 tablespoons unsalted butter
¼ cup honey

4 garlic cloves, minced
Salt

Freshly ground black pepper

1. Pour the water into the inner pot and place a steamer rack trivet in the bottom.

2. Arrange the carrots in a steamer basket. Place the basket on the trivet.

3. Close the lid and set the cooking time to 2 minutes at high/normal pressure. It will take 7 minutes to reach pressure.

4. Quick release the pressure. Remove the basket and trivet from the pot and set aside. Pour the water out of the pot.

5. Select the Sauté function. Melt the butter in the pot. Add the honey and stir until it's completely blended into the butter. Add the garlic and sauté, stirring, for 30 seconds. Add the carrots and toss. Sauté, stirring often, for about 6 minutes or until the sauce thickens slightly. Press Cancel.

6. Transfer the carrots and sauce to a serving platter and season with salt and pepper.

7. Store leftovers in an airtight container in the refrigerator.

Substitution Tip

This recipe can easily be made vegan by substituting margarine for the butter and maple syrup for the honey.

Per serving: Calories: 192; Fat: 9g; Protein: 1g; Carbohydrates: 29g; Fiber: 3g; Sugar: 23g; Sodium: 187mg

SIMPLE RICED CAULIFLOWER

› SERVES 4

› **Prep time:** 3 minutes

› **Pressure cook:** 1 minute High

› **Sauté:** 4 minutes

› **Release:** Quick

› **Total time:** 15 minutes

› 5-Ingredient, Super Quick

Cauliflower is a great, low-carb alternative to rice that also happens to be naturally high in fiber and B vitamins. Because it is surprisingly quick to prepare in the Instant Pot, making your own riced cauliflower is more convenient than you might think.

| 1 cup water | 4 cups chopped cauliflower | 2 tablespoons olive oil
Salt | Freshly ground black pepper |

1. Pour the water into the inner pot and place a steamer rack trivet in the bottom.

2. Arrange the cauliflower in a steamer basket. Place the basket on the trivet.

3. Close the lid and set the cooking time to 1 minute at high/normal pressure. It will take 6 to 7 minutes to reach pressure.

4. Quick release the pressure. Remove the basket and trivet from the pot and set aside. Pour the water out of the pot.

5. Select the Sauté function. Heat the oil in the pot. Add the cauliflower to the pot and sauté for 3 to 4 minutes while breaking the cauliflower into small rice-size pieces with a potato masher. Press Cancel and discard any bigger stem pieces.

6. Season with salt and pepper and serve.

7. Store leftovers in an airtight container in the refrigerator, or freeze in airtight resealable bags.

Variation Tip

You can turn this simple recipe into cilantro-lime riced cauliflower by sautéing with minced garlic during the final stage, then mixing chopped fresh cilantro and freshly squeezed lime juice into the cauliflower before serving.

Per serving: Calories: 86; Fat: 7g; Protein: 2g; Carbohydrates: 5g; Fiber: 2g; Sugar: 2g; Sodium: 71mg

CAJUN CREAMED CORN

> SERVES 6
> **Prep time:** 10 minutes
> **Pressure cook:** 3 minutes High
> **Sauté:** 5 minutes

> **Release:** Quick
> **Total time:** 30 minutes

If your idea from childhood of creamed corn was the gloppy stuff from a can, you're in for a surprise with this dish, properly known as *maque choux*. The vegetables get an extra kick from Cajun spices, and just a touch of cream smooths out the flavors and texture.

2½ cups frozen corn

½ cup chopped onion

⅓ cup chopped red bell pepper

2 garlic cloves, minced

1 jalapeño pepper, seeded and minced

½ teaspoon Cajun seasoning

½ teaspoon kosher salt, plus more if needed

½ cup chicken stock

2 tablespoons unsalted butter

¼ cup heavy (whipping) cream

1 small tomato, seeded and diced (about ¼ cup)

¼ cup thinly sliced scallions, green parts only

1. Combine the corn, onion, bell pepper, garlic, jalapeño, Cajun seasoning, salt, stock, and butter in the inner pot.

2. Close the lid and set the cooking time to 3 minutes at high/normal pressure. It will take 10 minutes to reach pressure.

3. Quick release the pressure. Remove the lid.

4. Select the Sauté function. Bring the liquid to a boil and simmer for 3 minutes. Add the cream and cook for 1 to 2 minutes until the cream has thickened slightly. Add the tomato and scallions and stir until warmed through. Press Cancel.

5. Store leftovers in an airtight container in the refrigerator.

Ingredient Tip

If you use a commercial Cajun spice blend, check to see if it contains salt. If so, omit the salt at the beginning of cooking and add at the end if necessary.

Per serving: Calories: 118; Fat: 7g; Protein: 3g; Carbohydrates: 15g; Fiber: 2g; Sugar: 2g; Sodium: 298mg

ROASTED SWEET POTATOES WITH BEETS AND ROSEMARY

› SERVES 2
› **Prep time:** 5 minutes
› **Pressure cook:** 6 minutes High

› **Release:** Quick
› **Total time:** 30 minutes
› 5-Ingredient

Beets and sweet potatoes are a great combination, especially when roasted. But they're so dense, they take a long time to cook, and it can be tricky to make sure they don't burn on the outside before the centers are done. Using the Instant Pot gives you a head start with the cooking, so the final roasting can be done in a flash.

1 cup water

2 small beets, halved and roots trimmed

1 small sweet potato

1 tablespoon olive oil

½ teaspoon kosher salt

2 teaspoons finely chopped fresh rosemary, thyme, or oregano

1. Preheat the oven to 400°F.

2. Pour the water into the inner pot and place a steamer rack trivet in the bottom.

3. Arrange the beets and sweet potato in a steamer basket. Place the basket on the trivet.

4. Close the lid and set the cooking time to 6 minutes at high/normal pressure. It will take 6 minutes to reach pressure.

5. Quick release the pressure. Remove the vegetables, then peel them and cut into 1-inch chunks. Place on a baking sheet. Drizzle with the olive oil and sprinkle with the salt. Gently toss to coat.

6. Roast the vegetables for 8 to 10 minutes or until cooked through and brown in spots on the outside. Remove from the oven and sprinkle with the rosemary. Return to the oven for 1 more minute. Store leftovers in an airtight container in the refrigerator.

Variation Tip

If you want to double the recipe, use twice as many of the same size vegetables.

Per serving: Calories: 164; Fat: 7g; Protein: 3g; Carbohydrates: 24g; Fiber: 5g; Sugar: 8g; Sodium: 204 mg

CURRIED QUINOA

> SERVES 6
> **Prep time:** 3 minutes
> **Pressure cook:** 1 minute High
> **Release:** Natural for 10 minutes, then
> Quick Release

> **Total time:** 25 minutes
> 5-Ingredient

Quinoa is another great hands-off side dish to prepare in the Instant Pot. It can be seasoned many ways, just like stovetop quinoa. Not only a side dish, this curried quinoa makes a great base for a Buddha bowl or stuffing for roasted peppers.

Nonstick cooking spray

1½ cups chicken stock

1 cup quinoa, rinsed well

1 tablespoon curry powder

1 teaspoon seasoning salt

¼ teaspoon garlic powder

1. Spray the inside of the inner pot with cooking spray. Combine the stock, quinoa, curry powder, seasoning salt, and garlic powder in the pot and stir gently.

2. Close the lid and set the cooking time to 1 minute at high/normal pressure. It will take 8 minutes to reach pressure.

3. Allow the pressure to release from the pot naturally for 10 minutes, then quick release the remaining pressure.

4. Open the lid, fluff with a fork, and serve.

5. Store leftovers in an airtight container in the refrigerator.

Substitution Tip

You can make this dish vegetarian by substituting vegetable stock or water for the chicken stock.

Per serving: Calories: 112; Fat: 2g; Protein: 5g; Carbohydrates: 19g; Fiber: 3g; Sugar: 0g; Sodium: 621mg

CREAMY MACARONI AND CHEESE

> SERVES 8
> **Prep time:** 5 minutes
> **Pressure cook:** 6 minutes High

> **Release:** Quick
> **Total time:** 25 minutes

Macaroni and cheese is so easy to cook in the Instant Pot that you won't want to make the boxed stuff again. This creamy recipe is a delicious basic mac and cheese. Feel free to use it as a starting point for a customized mac and cheese, using different cheeses and different toppings, such as bacon or ham.

4 cups water	½ teaspoon onion powder	1 pound dry elbow macaroni	2 cups shredded cheddar cheese
½ teaspoon salt	¼ teaspoon freshly ground black pepper	¾ cup milk	1 cup shredded Gouda cheese
½ teaspoon garlic powder			

1. Mix the water, salt, garlic powder, onion powder, and pepper together in the inner pot. Add the macaroni to the pot, making sure the noodles are mostly submerged, but do not stir.

2. Close the lid and set the cooking time to 6 minutes at high/normal pressure. It will take 10 to 11 minutes to reach pressure.

3. Quick release the pressure. Remove the lid. Gradually stir in the milk, cheddar cheese, and Gouda cheese, alternating between a little of the milk and a handful of cheese at a time, and stir until the cheeses are melted.

4. Serve hot.

Ingredient Tip

I have found the combination of cheddar cheese with a semi-soft or soft white cheese like Gouda to be pretty tried-and-true. You can experiment by substituting Monterey Jack, Gruyère, Havarti, or Muenster for the Gouda.

Per serving: Calories: 393; Fat: 15g; Protein: 18g; Carbohydrates: 44g; Fiber: 2g; Sugar: 3g; Sodium: 425mg

GREEK SALAD WITH BULGUR WHEAT

> SERVES 4
> **Prep time:** 10 minutes
> **Pressure cook:** 0 minutes High

> **Release:** Natural for 2 minutes, then Quick Release
> **Total time:** 25 minutes

This dish is my combination of Middle Eastern tabbouleh and Greek salad. It has more bulgur than a traditional tabbouleh, but it keeps the same bold use of parsley and mint. Cucumber, tomatoes, olives, and feta cheese come from the Greek side of the table. Together, the flavors and textures make a great side or light lunch dish.

- ½ cup coarse bulgur wheat
- ½ cup water
- ¼ teaspoon kosher salt
- ⅓ cup chopped cucumber
- ½ cup chopped cherry tomatoes
- 1 scallion, sliced, green parts only
- 2 tablespoons coarsely chopped Kalamata olives
- ¼ cup extra-virgin olive oil
- 2 tablespoons freshly squeezed lemon juice
- ⅓ cup crumbled feta cheese
- 1 tablespoon chopped fresh mint
- ¼ cup chopped fresh parsley

1. Pour the bulgur into the inner pot. Add the water and salt.

2. Close the lid and set the cooking time to 0 minutes at high/normal pressure. It will take 8 minutes to reach pressure.

3. Allow the pressure to release from the pot naturally for 2 minutes, then quick release the remaining pressure.

4. Open the lid and remove the pot. Fluff the bulgur with a fork and let cool for a few minutes. Transfer to a medium bowl.

5. Add the cucumber, tomatoes, scallion, and olives and toss to combine. Drizzle with the olive oil and lemon juice. Add the feta cheese, mint, and parsley and toss gently. Serve immediately.

Substitution Tip

You can make this recipe gluten-free by substituting cooked quinoa for the bulgur.

Per serving: Calories: 352; Fat: 32g; Protein: 6g; Carbohydrates: 14g; Fiber: 3g; Sugar: 2g; Sodium: 328mg

Easy Wonton Soup

Page 53

Chapter 4

Soups & Stews

CREAMY BROCCOLI CHEDDAR SOUP

> SERVES 4

> **Prep time:** 5 minutes

> **Pressure cook:** 2 minutes High

> **Release:** Quick

> **Total time:** 20 minutes

> One-Pot Meal, Super Quick

Thanks to the magic of the Instant Pot, this creamy, comforting soup is ready in about half the time it would take to cook it on the stovetop. The combination of cream and cheddar cheeses not only helps thicken the soup but also adds to its rich flavor and texture.

1 (32-ounce) carton chicken stock

3 cups chopped broccoli florets

½ teaspoon salt

¼ teaspoon freshly ground black pepper

¼ teaspoon garlic powder

¼ teaspoon onion powder

3 cups shredded cheddar cheese

8 ounces cream cheese, cubed, at room temperature

1. Pour the stock, broccoli, salt, pepper, garlic powder, and onion powder into the inner pot and stir.

2. Close the lid and set the cooking time to 2 minutes at high/normal pressure. It will take 12 minutes to reach pressure.

3. Quick release the pressure. Open the lid and gradually add the cheddar cheese and cream cheese to the pot, stirring until the cheeses have completely blended into the soup.

4. Store leftovers in an airtight container in the refrigerator.

Variation Tip

If you prefer a creamier soup, blend the soup with an immersion blender, or in a standard blender, working in batches.

Per serving: Calories: 576; Fat: 49g; Protein: 27g; Carbohydrates: 9g; Fiber: 2g; Sugar: 4g; Sodium: 821mg

MUSHROOM-LENTIL SOUP

> SERVES 4
> **Prep time:** 3 minutes
> **Sauté:** 4 minutes
> **Pressure cook:** 2 minutes High

> **Release:** Natural for 5 minutes, then Quick Release
> **Total time:** 30 minutes
> **One-Pot Meal**

This rich vegan soup is perfect on cold fall and winter days without feeling too heavy. Using canned lentils reduces the prep and cook time so you can be sipping your soup in in a flash. Lentils are a great source of fiber and protein, so add this dish to your Meatless Mondays recipe rotation.

1 tablespoon olive oil	3 cups sliced shiitake mushrooms	½ teaspoon salt	2 (15-ounce) cans lentils, drained and rinsed
½ medium onion, finely chopped	5 cups vegetable stock	¼ teaspoon freshly ground black pepper	¼ cup chopped scallions, green parts only
3 garlic cloves, minced	1 teaspoon dried thyme		

1. Select the Sauté function. Heat the oil in the inner pot. Add the onion and garlic to the pot and sauté for 1 minute. Add the mushrooms and sauté for about 3 minutes or until the mushrooms start to soften. Press Cancel.

2. Add the stock, thyme, salt, and pepper to the pot and stir with a wooden spoon, scraping the bottom of the pot to loosen any brown bits. Stir in the lentils.

3. Close the lid and set the cooking time to 2 minutes at high/normal pressure. It will take 16 minutes to reach pressure.

4. Allow the pressure to release from the pot naturally for 5 minutes, then quick release the remaining pressure.

5. Serve the soup in bowls, topped with the scallions. Store leftovers in an airtight container in the refrigerator.

Flavor Boost

Drizzle some sesame oil into each bowl to add savory flavor.

Per serving: Calories: 243; Fat: 4g; Protein: 14g; Carbohydrates: 39g; Fiber: 14g; Sugar: 6g; Sodium: 876mg

SHORTCUT BOUILLABAISSE

› SERVES 4 TO 6
› **Prep time:** 5 minutes
› **Pressure cook:** 3 minutes High
› **Sauté:** 6 minutes

› **Release:** Quick
› **Total time:** 30 minutes
› One-Pot Meal

Bouillabaisse is a seafood stew that originated in Marseille, France. Fisherman would make the stew with parts of fish they were unable to sell. Whereas traditional bouillabaisses cook low and slow with multiple types of bone-in fish, this shortcut version employs canned and boned seafood. Serve the stew with crusty bread to soak up every last drop of the fantastically flavorful broth.

3 cups fish stock

1 (14.5-ounce) can petite diced tomatoes, with juices

1 (10-ounce) can whole baby clams, drained

1 (8-ounce) package fresh cut onion, carrot, and celery blend

2 teaspoons minced garlic

1 teaspoon seasoning salt

½ teaspoon freshly ground black pepper

1 (6-ounce) can tiny shrimp, drained

1 pound cod, cut into 1-inch chunks

Chopped fresh parsley, for garnish

1. Pour the fish stock into the inner pot. Add the tomatoes with their juices, clams, vegetable blend, garlic, salt, and pepper to the pot and stir.

2. Close the lid and set the cooking time to 3 minutes at high/normal pressure. It will take 16 minutes to reach pressure.

3. Quick release the pressure. Open the lid and select the Sauté function. Add the shrimp to the pot. Use an immersion blender to puree the soup. Add the cod and simmer for about 5 minutes or until cooked. Press Cancel.

4. Serve in bowls, garnished with chopped parsley.

5. Store leftovers in an airtight container in the refrigerator.

Ingredient Tip

You can find precut vegetable blends in your grocer's produce section. Using precut fresh vegetables is a big time-saver for this recipe.

Per serving: Calories: 267; Fat: 3g; Protein: 42g; Carbohydrates: 15g; Fiber: 3g; Sugar: 7g; Sodium: 1,223mg

DUMP-AND-START CHICKEN AND RICE SOUP

> SERVES 6
> Prep time: 5 minutes
> Pressure cook: 3 minutes High

> Release: Natural for 5 minutes, then Quick Release
> Total time: 30 minutes
> One-Pot Meal

There are few things more comforting than a good chicken soup. My family prefers chicken and rice soup to chicken noodle soup, and the Instant Pot gave us a way to make it more easily and hands-off than ever. An optional squeeze of lemon takes the flavors over the edge, in a really good way.

5 cups chicken stock

1 cup water

2 (10-ounce) cans chunk chicken breast, drained

1 cup chopped carrot

1 cup chopped celery

⅔ cup long-grain white rice, well rinsed

1 tablespoon dried minced onion

1 teaspoon salt

½ teaspoon dried thyme

¼ teaspoon freshly ground black pepper

¼ teaspoon garlic powder

Lemon wedges, for serving (optional)

1. Pour the stock and water into the inner pot. Add the chicken, carrot, celery, rice, onion, salt, thyme, pepper, and garlic powder to the pot and stir.

2. Close the lid and set the cooking time to 3 minutes at high/normal pressure. It will take 16 minutes to reach pressure.

3. Allow the pressure to release from the pot naturally for 5 minutes, then quick release the remaining pressure.

4. Serve in bowls, with a squeeze of fresh lemon juice (if using).

5. Store leftovers in an airtight container in the refrigerator.

Variation Tip

If you have time, substitute 1 pound of cubed chicken breast meat for the canned and increase the pressure cooking time to 7 minutes.

Per serving: Calories: 213; Fat: 3g; Protein: 25g; Carbohydrates: 19g; Fiber: 1g; Sugar: 1g; Sodium: 473mg

CHICKEN TORTILLA SOUP

› SERVES 4 TO 6

› **Prep time:** 3 minutes

› **Pressure cook:** 7 minutes High

› **Release:** Quick

› **Total time:** 30 minutes

› **One-Pot Meal**

This dump-and-go soup is satisfying and oh-so-good. Using canned ingredients makes the preparation quick. I like to make this soup on busy days when I don't have a lot of time for prepping dinner.

3 (14.5-ounce) cans chicken broth

1 (15-ounce) can corn, drained

1 (15-ounce) can black beans, drained and rinsed

1 (10-ounce) can diced tomatoes with green chiles

½ teaspoon chili powder

½ teaspoon seasoning salt

½ teaspoon garlic powder

1 pound boneless skinless chicken breasts, cut into thirds

1 (3.5-ounce) package tortilla strips (used for salad toppings)

Shredded Mexican cheese blend, for garnish

Chopped fresh cilantro, for garnish

1. Pour the broth, corn, black beans, tomatoes with green chiles with their juices, chili powder, seasoning salt, and garlic powder into the inner pot. Add the chicken to the pot and stir.

2. Close the lid and set the cooking time to 7 minutes at high/normal pressure. It will take 17 minutes to reach pressure.

3. Quick release the pressure.

4. Open the lid. Using tongs, transfer the chicken from the pot to a plate. Use two forks to shred the chicken, then return the shredded chicken to the pot.

5. Ladle the soup into serving bowls and top with tortilla strips, shredded cheese, and cilantro.

CONTINUED →

6. Leftover soup can be stored in an airtight container in the refrigerator without the tortilla strips, cheese, and cilantro. Add the toppings to individual portions after reheating.

Flavor Boost

Feel free to experiment with additional toppings. My rule of thumb with this soup is that if a topping is good on a taco, it's also good on this soup. Avocado, sour cream, and red onion are tasty additions.

Per serving: Calories: 412; Fat: 10g; Protein: 36g; Carbohydrates: 48g; Fiber: 9g; Sugar: 2g; Sodium: 585mg

EASY WONTON SOUP

› SERVES 4
› **Prep time:** 5 minutes
› **Pressure cook:** 2 minutes High
› **Sauté:** 5 minutes

› **Release:** Quick
› **Total time:** 30 minutes
› One-Pot Meal

This soup is a family favorite that is on regular rotation in our home. The name says it all. The soup is surprisingly easy considering how tasty and filling it is. Using frozen mini wontons makes this a very hands-off dinner with minimal prep.

5 cups chicken stock

1 cup water

1 cup sliced shiitake mushrooms

1 tablespoon soy sauce

2 garlic cloves, crushed

1 teaspoon ginger paste

12 ounces frozen mini wontons

1 head bok choy, leaves stemmed and coarsely chopped

1 scallion, chopped, white and green parts

1½ teaspoons sesame oil

1. Pour the stock and water into the inner pot. Add the mushrooms, soy sauce, garlic, and ginger paste to the pot and stir.

2. Close the lid and set the cooking time to 2 minutes at high/normal pressure. It will take 14 minutes to reach pressure.

3. Quick release the pressure.

4. Open the lid and select the Sauté function. Add the frozen wontons and bok choy leaves to the pot. Sauté for 4 to 5 minutes or until the wontons float to the top and are cooked through. Press Cancel and stir in the scallion.

5. Serve drizzled with sesame oil.

6. Store leftovers in an airtight container in the refrigerator.

Flavor Boost

You can add to the flavor of this soup by trying different types of mini frozen wontons. I prefer the pork wontons, but you can also find chicken and different combinations of meats and vegetables.

Per serving: Calories: 164; Fat: 7g; Protein: 9g; Carbohydrates: 18g; Fiber: 4g; Sugar: 6g; Sodium: 614mg

ASOPAO DE POLLO (PUERTO RICAN-STYLE CHICKEN STEW)

› SERVES 4
› **Prep time:** 5 minutes
› **Sauté:** 3 minutes
› **Pressure cook:** 5 minutes High

› **Release:** Natural for 5 minutes, then Quick Release
› **Total time:** 30 minutes
› One-Pot Meal

Asopao is considered to be Puerto Rico's national dish. As with many traditional recipes, every family has its own way of making this comforting stew. This quick Instant Pot version gives you the comforting feeling and rich flavors when you're craving asopao but are short on time.

1 tablespoon olive oil

4 cups chicken stock

4 boneless, skinless chicken thighs, cut into 1-inch cubes

1½ teaspoons adobo seasoning, divided

½ cup sofrito (see tip)

1 (14.5-ounce) can diced tomatoes

⅔ cup long-grain white rice, well rinsed

½ cup pimiento-stuffed olives

1 tablespoon capers

1 teaspoon chicken bouillon

½ teaspoon dried oregano

¼ teaspoon freshly ground black pepper

¼ teaspoon ground cumin

1 cup canned peas (optional)

1. Select the Sauté function. Heat the oil in the inner pot. Pour the stock into a microwave-safe measuring cup and microwave on high power for 3 to 4 minutes or until hot.

2. Season the chicken with 1 teaspoon of adobo. Add the chicken to the pot and sauté for 2 minutes. Add the sofrito and sauté for 1 more minute. Press Cancel.

3. Pour the hot stock into the pot and stir with a wooden spoon, scraping the bottom of the pot to loosen any brown bits. Stir in the diced tomatoes with their juices, rice, olives, capers, bouillon, the remaining ½ teaspoon of adobo, the oregano, pepper, and cumin.

4. Close the lid and set the cooking time to 5 minutes at high/normal pressure. It will take 12 minutes to reach pressure.

5. Allow the pressure to release from the pot naturally for 5 minutes, then quick release the remaining pressure.

6. Open the lid and stir in the peas (if using).

7. Store leftovers in an airtight container in the refrigerator.

Ingredient Tip

You can find adobo seasoning and jarred sofrito in the international section of your grocery store, or you can use a homemade recipe for either. To add a little something extra to this dish, add a packet of *Sazón con Culantro y Achiote* as well.

Per serving: Calories: 382; Fat: 16g; Protein: 29g; Carbohydrates: 31g; Fiber: 4g; Sugar: 3g; Sodium: 819mg

HEARTY GROUND BEEF STEW

› **SERVES 6**
› **Prep time:** 5 minutes
› **Sauté:** 5 minutes
› **Pressure cook:** 5 minutes High

› **Release:** Quick
› **Total time:** 30 minutes
› One-Pot Meal

Stews often take longer to pressure cook than other recipes, but the use of ground beef means this rich beef stew cooks much faster. Save even more time by prepping your ingredients while the beef browns.

1 pound ground beef

1 medium
onion, chopped

2 cups beef
stock, heated

1 (14.5-ounce) can
Italian-seasoned
diced tomatoes,
drained

2 medium potatoes,
cut into 1-inch cubes

1 (8-ounce) can
tomato sauce

1 cup mini cut carrots

1 cup frozen peas

1 teaspoon salt

¼ teaspoon freshly
ground black pepper

¼ teaspoon
garlic powder

2 tablespoons
chopped
fresh parsley

1. Select the Sauté function. Put the beef and onion in the inner pot and sauté for 5 minutes, stirring occasionally.

2. Press Cancel and drain any excess oil from the pot.

3. Add the stock to the pot and stir with a wooden spoon, scraping the bottom of the pot to loosen any brown bits. Stir in the tomatoes, potatoes, tomato sauce, carrots, peas, salt, pepper, and garlic powder.

4. Close the lid and set the cooking time to 5 minutes at high/normal pressure. It will take 15 minutes to reach pressure.

5. Quick release the pressure. Open the lid and garnish with the parsley. Store leftovers in an airtight container in the refrigerator.

Flavor Boost

Add up to 1 tablespoon of Worcestershire sauce or 1 teaspoon of Italian seasoning.

Per serving: Calories: 200; Fat: 4g; Protein: 20g; Carbohydrates: 22g; Fiber: 5g; Sugar: 5g; Sodium: 469mg

WEEKNIGHT CHILE VERDE (GREEN CHILE PORK STEW)

> SERVES 4
> **Prep time:** 5 minutes
> **Sauté:** 5 minutes
> **Pressure cook:** 3 minutes High

> **Release:** Natural for 5 minutes, then Quick Release
> **Total time:** 30 minutes

This Mexican-inspired pork stew comes out super flavorful in your Instant Pot. I call this shortcut version of my longer-cooking chile verde "Weeknight Chile Verde" because it uses shortcuts like canned tomatillos and peppers and leftover or prepared carnitas meat. The stew is wonderful served with rice and beans or in tortillas as tacos.

1 tablespoon olive oil

1 (25-ounce) can whole tomatillos, drained

1 (7-ounce) can whole jalapeño peppers, drained

4 garlic cloves, peeled

½ medium onion, chopped

1 green bell pepper, seeded and chopped

1½ cups chicken stock

½ teaspoon dried oregano

½ teaspoon ground cumin

½ teaspoon salt

¼ teaspoon freshly ground black pepper

1 pound pork carnitas

¼ cup chopped fresh cilantro

1. Select the Sauté function. Heat the oil in the inner pot.

2. Puree the tomatillos, jalapeños, and garlic in a food processor or blender and set aside.

3. In the pot, sauté the onion and bell pepper for 3 minutes or until the vegetables begin to soften. Press Cancel.

4. Add the stock, oregano, cumin, salt, and pepper to the pot and stir with a wooden spoon, scraping the bottom of the pot to loosen any brown bits. Stir in the reserved tomatillo mixture.

5. Close the lid and set the cooking time to 3 minutes at high/normal pressure. It will take 12 minutes to reach pressure.

6. Allow the pressure to release from the pot naturally for 5 minutes, then quick release the remaining pressure.

7. Open the lid and select the Sauté function again. Stir in the carnitas and simmer for 2 minutes, then press Cancel. Serve garnished with the cilantro.

8. Store leftovers in an airtight container in the refrigerator.

Variation Tip

If you prefer to use fresh jalapeño peppers, you can use 2 or 3 seeded peppers in place of the canned peppers.

Per serving: Calories: 422; Fat: 26g; Protein: 31g; Carbohydrates: 17g; Fiber: 6g; Sugar: 10g; Sodium: 362mg

QUICK CAJUN-STYLE MEATBALL STEW

> SERVES 4
> **Prep time:** 5 minutes
> **Pressure cook:** 5 minutes High

> **Sauté:** 10 minutes
> **Release:** Quick
> **Total time:** 30 minutes

Meatball stew is a South Louisiana comfort food characterized by its dark roux–based gravy. This shortcut recipe will be your best friend on days when you don't have time to make a homemade dark roux. Using a prechopped vegetable blend for the "holy trinity" (the Cajun/Creole version of mirepoix) is another way to shorten prep time. Buy meatballs from the store or use your favorite meatball recipe, and serve this dish with rice.

3 cups beef
  stock, divided
1 pound ready-to-cook
  meatballs
½ cup jarred dark roux
2 tablespoons
  unsalted butter

1½ cups prechopped
  Creole vegetable
  mix with onion,
  celery, and bell
  pepper (optional
  garlic and scallions)

Hot sauce, for
  seasoning
Salt
Freshly ground
  black pepper

2 (15-ounce)
  cans sliced
  potatoes, drained
1 (14.5-ounce)
  can sliced
  carrots, drained

1. Pour 1 cup of stock into the inner pot and place a steamer rack trivet in the bottom. Arrange the meatballs on the trivet.

2. Close the lid and set the cooking time to 5 minutes at high/normal pressure. It will take 10 minutes to reach pressure.

3. Quick release the pressure. Remove the trivet and pour the broth with the meatball drippings into a medium bowl with the remaining 2 cups of stock. Whisk the roux into the stock until the roux is dissolved. Clean out the inner pot.

4. To make the gravy, select the Sauté function and melt the butter in the pot. Add the Creole vegetable mix and sauté for 6 to 8 minutes or until soft. Add the stock mixture and stir until smooth. Add hot sauce, salt, and pepper to taste.

5. Add the meatballs to the gravy and sauté for about 2 minutes, until the gravy has thickened. Press Cancel and stir in the potatoes and carrots.

6. Store the leftovers in an airtight container in the refrigerator.

Ingredient Tip

You can find prechopped vegetables in your grocery store produce section. The Cajun/Creole chopped veggie blend will include the "holy trinity" of onion, celery, and bell pepper, and sometimes garlic and scallions. If you can't find the prechopped blend, combine chopped onion, celery, and bell pepper with minced garlic for this recipe. If you can't find prepared dark roux, you can make your own by sautéing ¼ cup flour in 3 tablespoons of oil, stirring constantly until the roux turns chocolate brown (a minimum of 8 to 10 minutes).

Per serving: Calories: 539; Fat: 20g; Protein: 33g; Carbohydrates: 46g; Fiber: 10g; Sugar: 8g; Sodium: 1,189mg

Tortellini with Summer
Vegetables and Pesto

Page 66

Chapter 5

Meatless Mains

TRUFFLED MUSHROOM RISOTTO

› SERVES 6
› **Prep time:** 5 minutes
› **Sauté:** 6 minutes
› **Pressure cook:** 6 minutes High

› **Release:** Quick
› **Total time:** 30 minutes
› One-Pot Meal

If I had to pick one dish that made the purchase of an Instant Pot worthwhile, it would be risotto. Pressure cooking risotto is a game changer. No more standing over the stove, stirring constantly for 30 minutes; Instant Pot risotto is hands-off and perfect every time.

3 tablespoons unsalted butter

8 ounces sliced mushrooms

1 cup finely chopped onion

2 garlic cloves, minced

1½ cups arborio rice

½ cup dry white wine

3¼ cups vegetable broth

½ cup heavy (whipping) cream

½ teaspoon salt

¼ teaspoon freshly ground black pepper

½ cup shredded parmesan cheese

1 to 2 tablespoons truffle oil

1. Select the Sauté function. Melt the butter in the inner pot. Add the mushrooms, onion, and garlic to the pot and sauté for 3 minutes.

2. Add the rice and wine to the pot and stir well. Sauté for 2½ minutes, then stir in the broth, cream, salt, and pepper. Press Cancel.

3. Close the lid and set the cooking time to 6 minutes at high/normal pressure. It will take 11 minutes to reach pressure.

4. Quick release the pressure. Open the lid and add the parmesan cheese and truffle oil to taste. Stir until the cheese is melted. Let the risotto sit in the pot, uncovered, for 3 minutes to thicken before serving.

5. This is best served fresh and hot, but leftovers can be stored in an airtight container in the refrigerator.

Substitution Tip

If you prefer not to use heavy cream, you can use the same quantity of chicken stock in its place.

Per serving: Calories: 367; Fat: 18g; Protein: 8g; Carbohydrates: 44g; Fiber: 2g; Sugar: 2g; Sodium: 358mg

SPAGHETTI AL POMODORO (PASTA WITH TOMATO SAUCE)

> SERVES 4
> **Prep time:** 5 minutes
> **Sauté:** 1 minute
> **Pressure cook:** 8 minutes High

> **Release:** Quick
> **Total time:** 25 minutes
> One-Pot Meal

It's hard to believe that such a simple combination of ingredients can come together so deliciously in just 25 minutes, almost (thanks, Instant Pot magic). My family cheers when this recipe is on our dinner menu, and I hope it will become a family favorite for you, too.

1 (14-ounce) can whole peeled tomatoes	3 garlic cloves, crushed	½ teaspoon freshly ground black pepper	⅓ cup coarsely chopped fresh basil
2 tablespoons olive oil	2½ cups water	12 ounces spaghetti, broken in half	¼ cup shredded parmesan cheese
	1 teaspoon salt		

1. In a food processor, puree the tomatoes with their juices. Set aside.

2. Select the Sauté function. Heat the oil in the inner pot. Add the garlic to the pot and sauté for about 30 seconds until fragrant. Press Cancel.

3. Add the water, salt, and pepper to the pot and stir. Add the pasta to the pot, making sure the noodles are evenly submerged, but do not stir. Pour the pureed tomatoes over the pasta. Sprinkle the basil over the tomatoes.

4. Close the lid and set the cooking time to 8 minutes at high/normal pressure. It will take 9 minutes to reach pressure.

5. Quick release the pressure. Open the lid and add the parmesan cheese, stirring until the cheese has completely blended into the sauce and any noodles that were stuck together have broken up.

6. Store leftovers in an airtight container in the refrigerator.

Per serving: Calories: 421; Fat: 10g; Protein: 14g; Carbohydrates: 68g; Fiber: 5g; Sugar: 5g; Sodium: 714mg

TORTELLINI WITH SUMMER VEGETABLES AND PESTO

› **SERVES 4**
› **Prep time:** 5 minutes
› **Pressure cook:** 0 minutes High

› **Release:** Quick
› **Total time:** 25 minutes
› 5-Ingredient, One-Pot Meal

I love using pesto in recipes, because it's so full of flavor that you hardly need any other seasonings. It's a great solution when you need a fast and easy recipe. When tossed with some quick, pressure-cooked prepared tortellini and vegetables, you have a delicious dinner that's ideal for busy weeknights.

2 cups water

1 pound frozen cheese tortellini

1 yellow squash, cut into ½-inch rings, halved or quartered if large

1 zucchini, cut into ½-inch rings, halved or quartered if large

½ cup basil pesto

1 cup cherry or grape tomatoes, halved

1. Pour the water into the inner pot. Add the tortellini, then place the squash and zucchini on top.

2. Close the lid and set the cooking time to 0 minutes at high/normal pressure. It will take 16 minutes to reach pressure.

3. Quick release the pressure. Open the lid and strain the tortellini and vegetables through a colander, reserving ½ cup of the liquid. Transfer the pasta and vegetables to a large bowl.

4. In a small bowl, mix the reserved liquid with the pesto. Toss with the tortellini and vegetables, then stir in the tomatoes.

5. Store the leftovers in an airtight container in the refrigerator.

Variation Tip

Feel free to be flexible with the veggies. Broccoli and asparagus are fabulous alternatives and take the same amount of cooking time. You can also stir spinach into the tortellini with the tomatoes during the final step.

Per serving: Calories: 371; Fat: 8g; Protein: 17g; Carbohydrates: 58g; Fiber: 3g; Sugar: 4g; Sodium: 464mg

MUSHROOM RAGOUT

› SERVES 4
› **Prep time:** 5 minutes
› **Sauté:** 10 minutes
› **Pressure cook:** 2 minutes High

› **Release:** Quick
› **Total time:** 25 minutes
› One-Pot Meal

Inspired by the *New York Times* mushroom ragoût recipe by Martha Rose Shulman, this dish is a hearty and flavorful vegetarian stew that is wonderful served with pasta, polenta, or on its own with some crusty bread.

2 tablespoons olive oil	½ medium onion, chopped	2 cups vegetable stock	Pinch salt
1 pound sliced baby bella mushrooms	2 tablespoons all-purpose flour	1 teaspoon dried rosemary	Freshly ground black pepper
8 ounces sliced shiitake mushrooms	½ cup Marsala wine	1 teaspoon dried thyme	Chopped fresh parsley, for garnish

1. Select the Sauté function. Heat the oil in the inner pot. Add the bella and shiitake mushrooms and onion to the pot and sauté for 3 minutes or until the mushrooms start to sweat. Stir in the flour and sauté, stirring, for 2 minutes.

2. Pour the Marsala wine into the pot and stir with a wooden spoon, scraping the bottom of the pot to loosen any brown bits. Simmer for 5 minutes, stirring often. Press Cancel.

3. Add the stock, rosemary, thyme, salt, and pepper to the pot and stir.

4. Close the lid and set the cooking time to 2 minutes at high/normal pressure. It will take 7 minutes to reach pressure.

5. Quick release the pressure. Serve garnished with parsley.

6. Store leftovers in an airtight container in the refrigerator.

Ingredient Tip

I like purchasing presliced mushrooms to save prep time, but you can buy whole mushrooms and slice them.

Per serving: Calories: 171; Fat: 7g; Protein: 4g; Carbohydrates: 17g; Fiber: 3g; Sugar: 7g; Sodium: 112mg

HEARTY VEGAN CHILI

› SERVES 6
› **Prep time:** 5 minutes
› **Sauté:** 3 minutes
› **Pressure cook:** 5 minutes High

› **Release:** Quick
› **Total time:** 30 minutes
› One-Pot Meal

You won't miss the meat in this satisfying chili. Not just hearty, this vegan chili is rich in protein and fiber. Add this dish to your Meatless Monday menu when the weather turns cool, because it's the perfect recipe to warm and fill you up.

2 tablespoons olive oil

1 red bell pepper, seeded and chopped

½ cup prechopped onion

½ cup prechopped celery

2 teaspoons minced garlic

1 (28-ounce) can diced tomatoes, with their juices

2 (15-ounce) cans black beans, drained and rinsed

1 (15-ounce) can kidney beans, drained and rinsed

1½ cups vegetable stock

1 (10-ounce) pack plant-based ground meat substitute

2 tablespoons chili powder

2 teaspoons ground cumin

1½ teaspoons paprika

1 teaspoon dried oregano

½ teaspoon salt

1. Select the Sauté function. Heat the oil in the inner pot. Add the bell pepper, onion, and celery to the pot and sauté for 2 minutes. Stir in the garlic and sauté for 1 more minute. Press Cancel.

2. Add the tomatoes with their juices, black beans, kidney beans, stock, meat substitute, chili powder, cumin, paprika, oregano, and salt to the pot and stir, scraping the bottom of the pot with a wooden spoon to loosen any brown bits.

3. Close the lid and set the cooking time to 5 minutes at high/normal pressure. It will take 16 minutes to reach pressure.

4. Quick release the pressure.

5. Store leftovers in an airtight container in the refrigerator.

Variation Tip

If you prefer a less spicy chili, reduce the chili powder to 1 tablespoon.

Per serving: Calories: 350; Fat: 10g; Protein: 23g; Carbohydrates: 44g; Fiber: 17g; Sugar: 6g; Sodium: 693mg

VEGETARIAN BURRITO BOWLS

> SERVES 4
> **Prep time:** 5 minutes
> **Pressure cook:** 3 minutes High

> **Release:** Natural for 10 minutes, then Quick Release
> **Total time:** 30 minutes
> One-Pot Meal

Rice is already quick and easy to prepare in the Instant Pot. Combine it with a few canned ingredients and Tex-Mex spices, and you've got a delicious, dump-and-start one-pot meal.

- 1 (15-ounce) can corn, drained
- 1 (15-ounce) can black beans, drained and rinsed
- 1 (10-ounce) can diced tomatoes with green chiles
- 1 cup rice, well rinsed
- ½ cup vegetable stock
- 1 tablespoon freshly squeezed lime juice
- ½ teaspoon seasoning salt
- ½ teaspoon chili powder
- ¼ teaspoon garlic powder
- 1 medium avocado, chopped
- ¼ cup salsa
- 2 tablespoons chopped fresh cilantro
- ¼ cup shredded Mexican cheese blend (optional)
- ¼ cup sour cream (optional)

1. Combine the corn, black beans, diced tomatoes with green chiles and their juices, rice, stock, lime juice, seasoning salt, chili powder, and garlic powder in the inner pot and stir.

2. Close the lid and set the cooking time to 3 minutes at high/normal pressure. It will take 9 minutes to reach pressure.

3. Allow the pressure to release from the pot naturally for 10 minutes, then quick release the remaining pressure. Open the lid and stir the rice. Serve topped with avocado, salsa, cilantro, and cheese and sour cream (if using).

4. Leftovers can be stored without the avocado, salsa, cilantro, cheese, and sour cream in an airtight container in the refrigerator. Add the toppings to individual portions after reheating.

Flavor Boost

To add a little something extra, top with grilled fajita vegetables (onion and a few different colors of bell pepper).

Per serving: Calories: 423; Fat: 13g; Protein: 9g; Carbohydrates: 76g; Fiber: 13g; Sugar: 3g; Sodium: 571mg

SPICY TOFU CURRY

> SERVES 4
> **Prep time:** 10 minutes
> **Sauté:** 3 minutes

> **Pressure cook:** 4 minutes High
> **Release:** Quick
> **Total time:** 25 minutes

You might be surprised to learn, as I was, that tofu cooks very quickly in the Instant Pot. This spicy dish can be finished in the time it takes to make rice to serve with it. Meatless Mondays don't get easier or more delicious than this!

1 tablespoon extra-virgin olive oil	½ teaspoon kosher salt, divided	1 tablespoon freshly squeezed lime juice	1 pound firm or extra-firm tofu, drained and cut into ½-inch cubes
1 medium onion, chopped	¾ cup vegetable stock	1 teaspoon Thai red curry paste	
	2 tablespoons tomato paste	1 teaspoon curry powder	2 cups cooked white rice
3 garlic cloves, finely minced	1 (14-ounce) can diced tomatoes, drained	1 teaspoon sugar	2 scallions, sliced, green parts only
1 small red bell pepper, seeded and chopped			

1. Select the Sauté function. Heat the oil in the inner pot. Add the onion, garlic, and red bell pepper and sprinkle with ¼ teaspoon of salt. Cook for 2 to 3 minutes, stirring frequently, until the onion begins to soften. Press Cancel.

2. Stir in the stock, tomato paste, and tomatoes, scraping the bottom of the pot with a wooden spoon to loosen any brown bits. Stir until the tomato paste is blended into the sauce, then add the lime juice, curry paste, curry powder, and sugar and stir to combine. Add the tofu.

3. Close the lid and set the cooking time to 4 minutes at high/normal pressure. It will take 5 minutes to reach pressure.

4. Quick release the pressure. Open the lid and stir the curry. Allow the curry to sit for 2 to 3 minutes before serving over rice and garnishing with the scallions.

5. Store leftovers in an airtight container in the refrigerator.

Ingredient Tip

Don't want to waste the leftover tomato paste from a can? Scoop tablespoon-size portions onto wax paper, then freeze until solid. Store the frozen portions in an airtight container in the freezer.

Per serving: Calories: 343; Fat: 10g; Protein: 15g; Carbohydrates: 52g; Fiber: 5g; Sugar: 8g; Sodium: 341mg

LENTIL TACOS

> SERVES 6
> **Prep time:** 5 minutes
> **Pressure cook:** 7 minutes High

> **Release:** Natural for 5 minutes, then Quick Release
> **Total time:** 25 minutes

Is it Taco Tuesday or Meatless Monday? Either way, these vegetarian tacos will hit the spot. Taco-seasoned lentils cook in the Instant Pot before being added to taco shells with your favorite taco toppings. You won't miss the meat in this family-friendly dinner.

2 cups vegetable stock

1 cup dried brown or green lentils, rinsed

1 tablespoon chili powder

1½ teaspoons ground cumin

1 teaspoon seasoning salt

½ teaspoon dried oregano

¼ teaspoon garlic powder

12 taco shells

Optional toppings:

1½ cups shredded lettuce

1 cup salsa

1 cup shredded Mexican cheese blend

¾ cup finely chopped red onion

½ cup sour cream

Guacamole

Black olives, sliced

Tomatoes, chopped

Black beans

1. Pour the stock into the inner pot. Add the lentils, chili powder, cumin, seasoning salt, oregano, and garlic powder to the pot and stir.

2. Close the lid and set the cooking time to 7 minutes at high/normal pressure. It will take 8 minutes to reach pressure.

3. Allow the pressure to release from the pot naturally for 5 minutes, then quick release the remaining pressure.

4. Open the lid and transfer the lentils to a serving dish.

5. Serve on taco shells with your favorite taco toppings.

6. Leftover seasoned lentils can be stored in an airtight container in the refrigerator.

Ingredient Tip

This recipe yields lentils with a firmer texture. For softer lentils, increase the pressure cooking time by 1 minute.

Per serving: Calories: 240; Fat: 6g; Protein: 10g; Carbohydrates: 37g; Fiber: 6g; Sugar: 1g; Sodium: 123mg

MEDITERRANEAN-INSPIRED COUSCOUS-STUFFED EGGPLANT

› SERVES 2
› **Prep time:** 5 minutes
› **Pressure cook:** 2 minutes High
› **Sauté:** 5 minutes

› **Release:** Natural for 10 minutes, then Quick Release
› **Total time:** 30 minutes
› One-Pot Meal

This vegetarian variation of stuffed eggplant has a light and tasty Mediterranean-flavored filling that is prepared easily in the Instant Pot and served in a halved eggplant shell. Save any extra couscous filling to use on salads—or to eat on its own.

Nonstick cooking spray

1¾ cups vegetable stock

1 cup couscous

1 eggplant, halved lengthwise

1 tablespoon extra-virgin olive oil

½ red bell pepper, seeded and chopped

1 teaspoon dried oregano

½ teaspoon minced garlic

½ teaspoon salt

¼ teaspoon freshly ground black pepper

½ cup coarsely chopped canned marinated artichoke hearts, drained

½ cup crumbled feta cheese

⅓ cup halved grape tomatoes

⅓ cup chopped Kalamata olives

1 tablespoon freshly squeezed lemon juice

1. Spray the inside of the inner pot with cooking spray. Pour the stock into the pot. Add the couscous, making sure it's all submerged in the liquid, but do not stir.

2. Close the lid and set the cooking time to 2 minutes at high/normal pressure. It will take 6 minutes to reach pressure.

3. While the couscous cooks, scoop the flesh out of each eggplant half, leaving about ¼ inch of flesh around the edge, so the skin becomes a bowl. Chop the flesh into ½-inch cubes.

4. Allow the pressure to release from the pot naturally for 10 minutes, then quick release the remaining pressure.

5. Open the pot lid, fluff the couscous with a fork, and transfer it to a bowl. Clean out the inner pot.

6. Select the Sauté function. Heat the oil in the pot. Add the chopped eggplant flesh, bell pepper, and oregano to the pot and sauté for 3 minutes. Stir in the garlic, salt, and black pepper and sauté for 1 more minute. Press Cancel and stir in the couscous, artichoke hearts, feta, tomatoes, olives, and lemon juice.

7. Stuff the couscous mixture into the eggplant shells to serve.

8. Store leftover filling in an airtight container in the refrigerator.

Substitution Tip

You can make this meal gluten-free by substituting quinoa for the couscous. Just reduce the vegetable stock to 1½ cups, and pressure cook for 1 minute with a 10-minute natural release.

Per serving: Calories: 616; Fat: 19g; Protein: 21g; Carbohydrates: 94g; Fiber: 16g; Sugar: 14g; Sodium: 924mg

JACKFRUIT SLOPPY JOES

> SERVES 4 TO 6
> **Prep time:** 5 minutes
> **Pressure cook:** 5 minutes High

> **Release:** Natural for 10 minutes, then Quick Release
> **Total time:** 30 minutes

For a simple meal, enjoy these tangy, sweet, and satisfying sandwiches any day of the week. When served on gluten-free buns, this dish becomes a gluten-free meal. We love it with pickled jalapenos and red cabbage on top and some baked beans on the side.

- 2 (20-ounce) cans young green jackfruit, drained
- 1 cup vegetable stock
- ½ medium onion, diced
- ½ green bell pepper, seeded and diced
- ¼ cup tomato sauce
- 2 garlic cloves, minced
- 1 tablespoon gluten-free vegan Worcestershire sauce
- 1 tablespoon maple syrup
- 1 teaspoon ground cumin
- Freshly ground black pepper
- Salt (optional)
- 8 to 12 gluten-free hamburger buns

1. In the inner pot, break up the jackfruit using a potato masher or two forks. Add the stock, onion, bell pepper, tomato sauce, garlic, Worcestershire sauce, maple syrup, and cumin. Season to taste with black pepper and salt (if using) and stir to combine.

2. Close the lid and set the cooking time to 5 minutes at high/normal pressure. It will take 8 minutes to reach pressure.

3. Allow the pressure to release from the pot naturally for 10 minutes, then quick release the remaining pressure. Open the lid and stir the mixture, breaking up any remaining large pieces of jackfruit. Adjust the seasoning to taste.

4. Lightly toast the buns. Serve a heaping ¼ cup of sloppy joe mixture on each bun.

5. Leftover seasoned jackfruit can be stored in an airtight container in the refrigerator.

Variation Tip

For a higher protein meal, substitute two 15-ounce cans of lentils for the jackfruit or use one can of lentils and one can of jackfruit.

Per serving: Calories: 509; Fat: 5g; Protein: 13g; Carbohydrates: 109g; Fiber: 6g; Sugar: 59g; Sodium: 471mg

Orange Chicken

Page 92

Chapter 6

Seafood & Poultry

MUSSELS WITH RED PEPPER-GARLIC SAUCE

› SERVES 4
› **Prep time:** 10 minutes
› **Sauté:** 1 minute
› **Pressure cook:** 1 minute High

› **Release:** Quick
› **Total time:** 25 minutes

There's something so comforting about digging into a big bowl of steamed mussels with a savory broth. In this impressive but easy recipe, the roasted red pepper gives a hint of sweetness to the broth, which complements the mussels perfectly. Serve this with plenty of crusty bread for sopping up every last drop of the fabulous broth.

1 tablespoon extra-virgin olive oil	1 large roasted red bell pepper, minced or puréed	⅛ teaspoon red pepper flakes	2 tablespoons heavy (whipping) cream
4 garlic cloves, minced	¾ cup fish stock	3 pounds mussels, scrubbed and debearded	3 tablespoons coarsely chopped fresh parsley
	½ cup dry white wine		

1. Select the Sauté function. Heat the oil in the inner pot. Add the garlic and sauté for 30 seconds to 1 minute or until fragrant. Add the bell pepper, stock, wine, and red pepper flakes. Stir to combine. Press Cancel. Add the mussels to the pot.

2. Close the lid and set the cooking time to 1 minute at high/normal pressure. It will take 9 minutes to reach pressure.

3. Quick release the pressure. Open the lid and check the mussels; if they have not opened, replace the lid but don't lock it into place. Let the mussels steam for another 1 minute, until they've opened. (Discard any that do not open.)

4. Stir in the cream and parsley and serve with the cooking liquid. Serve hot.

Substitution Tip

If you don't have fish stock or can't find it, you can substitute clam juice or water in its place.

Per serving: Calories: 388; Fat: 14g; Protein: 41g; Carbohydrates: 17g; Fiber: 1g; Sugar: 2g; Sodium: 980mg

LEMON-CAPER POACHED HALIBUT

› SERVES 4
› **Prep time:** 5 minutes
› **Sauté:** 4 minutes
› **Pressure cook:** 3 minutes High

› **Release:** Quick
› **Total time:** 20 minutes
› Super Quick

This recipe is light but full of flavor. Fish steams beautifully and quickly in the Instant Pot, leaving you with moist, flavor-infused fillets. This recipe is quick enough that it works for lunch or dinner. Serve it with its sauce over orzo, or with some crusty bread for dipping.

1 tablespoon olive oil

2 garlic cloves, minced

½ cup dry white wine

2 cups chicken stock

½ cup chopped
   fresh parsley

3 tablespoons
   freshly squeezed
   lemon juice

1 tablespoon capers

1 pound halibut, cut
   into 4 fillets

½ teaspoon
   dried oregano

¼ teaspoon dried dill

Salt

Freshly ground
   black pepper

1. Select the Sauté function. Heat the oil in the inner pot. Add the garlic and sauté for 30 seconds to 1 minute or until fragrant. Pour the wine into the pot and simmer for 3 minutes. Press Cancel.

2. Stir in the stock, parsley, lemon juice, and capers. Place the halibut fillets in the pot. Season the fish with the oregano and dill, then add salt and pepper.

3. Close the lid and set the cooking time to 3 minutes at high/normal pressure. It will take 7 to 8 minutes to reach pressure.

4. Quick release the pressure. Open the lid and serve the fish in shallow bowls with the lemon-caper sauce.

5. Store leftovers in an airtight container in the refrigerator.

Variation Tip

If you're not a fan of halibut, this recipe also works well with flounder, cod, or haddock.

Per serving: Calories: 166; Fat: 5g; Protein: 21g; Carbohydrates: 3g; Fiber: 1g; Sugar: 0g; Sodium: 171mg

STEAMED COD WITH GINGER-GARLIC BROTH AND SNOW PEAS

> SERVES 4
> **Prep time:** 5 minutes
> **Pressure cook:** 2 minutes Low

> **Release:** Quick
> **Total time:** 20 minutes
> One-Pot Meal, Super Quick

Steamed whole fish topped with a flavorful mixture of vegetables, herbs, and spices is a classic Chinese-style dish, but a whole fish isn't always practical for the home cook. Fillets to the rescue! This recipe combines fish fillets and crunchy snow peas with a delicious, aromatic broth for an easy adaptation of the classic.

4 (6- to 8-ounce) cod fillets	1 cup fish stock or vegetable stock	2 tablespoons dry sherry	8 ounces snow peas, trimmed
¼ teaspoon kosher salt	2 tablespoons rice vinegar	1 tablespoon minced peeled fresh ginger	2 scallions, thinly sliced, green parts only
¼ teaspoon freshly ground black pepper	2 tablespoons soy sauce	1 tablespoon minced garlic	1 tablespoon toasted sesame oil

1. Season the cod on both sides with the salt and pepper. Combine the stock, vinegar, soy sauce, sherry, ginger, and garlic in the inner pot. Place a steamer rack trivet in the bottom and put the cod fillets on the trivet. Scatter the snow peas over the fish.

2. Close the lid and set the cooking time to 2 minutes at low pressure. It will take 7 to 8 minutes to reach pressure.

3. Quick release the pressure. Open the lid and carefully and remove the trivet from the pot.

4. With a large slotted spatula, divide the fish and snow peas among four shallow bowls. Spoon the broth over the fish. Top with the scallions and drizzle with the sesame oil. Store leftovers in an airtight container in the refrigerator.

Ingredient Tip

If you want to use frozen fish, increase the cooking time to 3 minutes.

Per serving: Calories: 318; Fat: 6g; Protein: 56g; Carbohydrates: 7g; Fiber: 2g; Sugar: 3g; Sodium: 871mg

CHICKEN AND ORZO WITH LEMON SAUCE

> SERVES 4
> **Prep time:** 5 minutes
> **Pressure cook:** 4 minutes Low
> **Sauté:** 2 minutes

> **Release:** Natural for 5 minutes, then Quick Release
> **Total time:** 30 minutes
> 5-Ingredient, One-Pot Meal

Based on the classic Greek soup avgolemono, this light pasta and chicken dish is as quick to prepare as it is delicious to eat. The lemony sauce is thickened with egg, resulting in a dish that's somewhere between stew and soup. Cooking the chicken breasts whole keeps them moist and tender.

4 cups chicken stock, plus more as necessary

6 ounces orzo

2 large boneless, skinless chicken breasts

¼ teaspoon kosher salt, plus more as necessary

1 large egg

2 tablespoons freshly squeezed lemon juice

Freshly ground black pepper

1. Pour the stock into the inner pot and stir in the orzo. Place the chicken breasts on top of the orzo and sprinkle them with the salt.

2. Close the lid and set the cooking time to 4 minutes at low pressure. It will take 12 minutes to reach pressure.

3. Allow the pressure to release from the pot naturally for 5 minutes, then quick release the remaining pressure.

4. Open the lid and transfer the chicken breasts to a cutting board. Let cool for a minute, then cut into bite-size pieces. Don't worry if the center of the chicken isn't quite done; it will cook again. While the chicken is cooling, thoroughly beat the egg in a small bowl. Whisk in the lemon juice.

5. Select the Sauté function. Slowly add about 1 cup of warm chicken stock to the egg and lemon mixture, whisking constantly. (If there is not enough stock in the pot to ladle out 1 cup, add more stock and bring it to a simmer.) Add the chicken pieces and simmer for 1 to 2 minutes or until the chicken is fully cooked. Press Cancel. Add the egg-and-stock mixture to the pot. Stir to combine. Adjust the seasoning if necessary, then serve.

6. Store leftovers in an airtight container in the refrigerator.

Substitution Tip

For a gluten-free version, you can substitute quinoa for the orzo. Adjust the cooking time to 1 minute at high pressure with a 10-minute natural release.

Per serving: Calories: 310; Fat: 8g; Protein: 32g; Carbohydrates: 32g; Fiber: 2g; Sugar: 0g; Sodium: 834mg

SESAME SOY CHICKEN WINGS

› SERVES 4
› **Prep time:** 5 minutes
› **Pressure cook:** 10 minutes High

› **Sauté:** 8 minutes
› **Release:** Quick
› **Total time:** 30 minutes

Although frying or roasting chicken wings produces wonderful, crispy skin, it's a messy and time-consuming business. Instead, for velvety meat that practically falls off the bone, try braising your chicken wings in a savory soy-based broth. One taste and you'll forget all about Buffalo wings!

1½ cups water, plus more as needed	2 or 3 slices peeled fresh ginger	1 teaspoon Chinese five-spice powder	2 tablespoons minced fresh cilantro
½ cup soy sauce	3 garlic cloves, lightly smashed	24 wing segments (drumettes and/ or flats)	
2 tablespoons toasted sesame oil	2 tablespoons sugar		

1. Pour the water and soy sauce into the inner pot. Add the sesame oil, ginger, garlic, sugar, and five-spice powder and stir to combine. Add the chicken wings and stir to coat with the liquid. The wings should be mostly submerged; if necessary, add a little more water.

2. Close the lid and set the cooking time to 10 minutes at high/normal pressure. It will take 6 minutes to reach pressure.

3. Quick release the pressure. Open the lid and use a slotted spoon to transfer the wings to a plate. Set aside.

4. Select the Sauté function. Bring the sauce to a boil and let it reduce by about half, about 8 minutes. Return the wings to the sauce and stir to coat. Press Cancel.

5. Transfer the wings to a serving bowl and pour the sauce over. Garnish with cilantro.

6. Store leftovers in an airtight container in the refrigerator.

Per serving: Calories: 297; Fat: 21g; Protein: 18g; Carbohydrates: 9g; Fiber: 7g; Sugar: 6g; Sodium: 1,797mg

CHICKEN MARSALA

> SERVES 4
> **Prep time:** 5 minutes
> **Sauté:** 10 minutes
> **Pressure cook:** 8 minutes High

> **Release:** Quick
> **Total time:** 30 minutes
> One-Pot Meal

Chicken Marsala is a classic dish with a simple formula: Chicken breasts are dredged in flour and sautéed before being served with a Marsala wine and garlic reduction. This quick Instant Pot version produces uber-tender chicken.

2 boneless, skinless chicken breasts, halved vertically to create 4 thin pieces

Salt

Freshly ground black pepper

¼ cup all-purpose flour

2 tablespoons olive oil

8 ounces sliced mushrooms

1 teaspoon minced garlic

½ cup Marsala wine

1 cup chicken stock

2 tablespoons unsalted butter

Chopped fresh parsley, for garnish

1. Season both sides of the chicken with salt and pepper. Pour the flour into a shallow dish and dredge the chicken in the flour.

2. Select the Sauté function. Heat the oil in the inner pot. Add the chicken to the pot and sauté for 2 minutes on each side. Transfer the chicken from the pot to a plate and set aside.

3. Add the mushrooms and garlic to the pot and sauté for 30 seconds. Pour the Marsala wine into the pot and stir with a wooden spoon, scraping the bottom of the pot to loosen any brown bits. Simmer for 5 minutes, stirring often. Press Cancel.

4. Stir in the stock, then place the chicken on top of the broth and mushroom mixture.

5. Close the lid and set the cooking time to 8 minutes at high/normal pressure. It will take 5 minutes to reach pressure.

6. Quick release the pressure. Open the lid and stir in the butter. Garnish with parsley. Store leftovers in an airtight container in the refrigerator.

Substitution Tip

Use Madeira, port, sherry, or dry white wine in place of the Marsala wine.

Per serving: Calories: 251; Fat: 14g; Protein: 22g; Carbohydrates: 8g; Fiber: 1g; Sugar: 1g; Sodium: 64mg

TUNA NOODLE CASSEROLE

› SERVES 4
› **Prep time:** 5 minutes
› **Sauté:** 8 minutes
› **Pressure cook:** 5 minutes Low

› **Release:** Quick
› **Total time:** 25 minutes
› One-Pot Meal

Tuna noodle casserole, despite its name, is actually better cooked in an Instant Pot than baked in a casserole dish, which can produce overcooked noodles and dried-out tuna. This version is rich and creamy, with a tangy hint from the sour cream.

1 tablespoon
  vegetable oil
1 cup chopped onion
½ cup chopped celery
6 ounces wide
  egg noodles

1 (12-ounce) can
  evaporated
  milk, divided
1 cup water
1 bay leaf
1 teaspoon kosher salt

1 large egg
1 teaspoon cornstarch
2 (5- to 6-ounce) cans
  tuna, drained
1 cup frozen
  peas, thawed

2 tablespoons
  sour cream
1 tablespoon heavy
  (whipping) cream

1. Select the Sauté function. Heat the oil in the inner pot. Add the onion and celery and cook for about 1 minute, stirring frequently, until softened. Press Cancel.

2. Add the noodles, ¾ cup of evaporated milk, the water, bay leaf, and salt to the pot. Stir to combine and submerge the noodles in the liquid.

3. Close the lid and set the cooking time to 5 minutes at low pressure. It will take 7 minutes to reach pressure.

4. Quick release the pressure. Open the lid. In a small bowl, whisk together the remaining ¾ cup of evaporated milk, the egg, and cornstarch. (You can do this while the noodles cook.)

5. Select the Sauté function again and adjust to low heat. Pour the milk mixture into the noodles and cook, stirring, until the sauce has thickened. Add the tuna and peas and stir gently. Let the tuna and peas heat for 1 to 2 minutes, then stir in the sour cream and heavy cream. Serve.

6. Store leftovers in an airtight container in the refrigerator.

Per serving: Calories: 450; Fat: 22g; Protein: 35g; Carbohydrates: 29g; Fiber: 3g; Sugar: 13g; Sodium: 772mg

GARLIC AND HERB CHICKEN THIGHS

> SERVES 4
> **Prep time:** 2 minutes
> **Sauté:** 4 minutes
> **Pressure cook:** 12 minutes High

> **Release:** Natural for 5 minutes, then Quick Release
> **Total time:** 30 minutes
> 5-Ingredient

I find dark meat to be juicier and more flavorful than chicken breasts. In the Instant Pot you can sear and pressure cook the chicken, all in the same pot, for a crispy skin on the outside and tender meat on the inside.

2 tablespoons unsalted butter

4 bone-in, skin-on chicken thighs

2 teaspoons Italian seasoning

Salt

Freshly ground black pepper

1 cup chicken stock

1 teaspoon minced garlic

1. Select the Sauté function. Melt the butter in the pot.

2. Season both sides of the chicken with the Italian seasoning and some salt and pepper. Add the chicken to the pot and sauté for 2 minutes per side or until brown. Transfer the chicken from the pot to a plate and set aside.

3. Pour the stock into the pot and stir with a wooden spoon, scraping the bottom of the pot to loosen any brown bits.

4. Place a steamer rack trivet in the bottom of the pot, and then place the chicken thighs on the trivet, skin-side up. Rub the garlic on top of the skin.

5. Close the lid and set the cooking time to 12 minutes at high/normal pressure. It will take 7 minutes to reach pressure.

6. Allow the pressure to release from the pot naturally for 5 minutes, then quick release the remaining pressure.

7. Remove the chicken and trivet. If desired, use the broth and drippings in the bottom of the pot to make a simple gravy.

8. Store leftovers in an airtight container in the refrigerator.

Per serving: Calories: 480; Fat: 38g; Protein: 32g; Carbohydrates: 1g; Fiber: 0g; Sugar: 0g; Sodium: 196mg

SHRIMP BOIL

> SERVES 4
> **Prep time:** 5 minutes
> **Pressure cook:** 7 minutes High

> **Release:** Quick
> **Total time:** 30 minutes
> One-Pot Meal

Shrimp boil is so fast and easy to make in the Instant Pot that you don't have to wait for a special occasion to serve it. I give the potatoes a head start so they can get nice and tender, and then add frozen shrimp toward the end so they don't overcook. If you're using fresh shrimp, shorten the cook time in step 4 to 1 minute.

1 cup chicken stock	4 links Cajun-style	1 tablespoon Cajun	¼ cup chopped
1 pound baby red	sausage, sliced	seasoning	fresh parsley
potatoes, halved	4 ears fresh corn,	1 pound frozen	1 lemon, cut
	shucked and halved	peel-and-eat shrimp	into wedges
	crosswise		

1. Combine the stock, potatoes, sausage, corn, and Cajun seasoning in the inner pot.

2. Close the lid and set the cooking time to 5 minutes at high/normal pressure. It will take 12 minutes to reach pressure.

3. Quick release the pressure. Open the lid and add the shrimp.

4. Close the lid again and set the cooking time to 2 minutes at high/normal pressure. It will take 6 minutes to reach pressure.

5. Quick release the pressure once more. Open the lid and stir in the parsley. Serve with the lemon wedges.

6. Ideally, this is best served fresh, but leftovers can be stored in an airtight container in the refrigerator.

Substitution Tip

For a pescatarian version of this recipe, use 2 pounds of shrimp, omit the sausage, and swap the chicken stock for low-sodium vegetable stock.

Per serving: Calories: 615; Fat: 31g; Protein: 42g; Carbohydrates: 46g; Fiber: 6g; Sugar: 6g; Sodium: 744mg

ORANGE CHICKEN

> SERVES 6
> **Prep time:** 5 minutes
> **Sauté:** 8 minutes

> **Pressure cook:** 6 minutes High
> **Release:** Quick
> **Total time:** 30 minutes

This sweet and tangy chicken dish is quicker than takeout, but you'll love it just as much. You can serve it with white, brown, or fried rice, or even additional stir-fried or steamed vegetables. The leftovers are also delicious the next day after the flavors have had time to steep—just store them in an airtight container and keep in the fridge.

4 tablespoons cornstarch, divided	1½ pounds boneless, skinless chicken thighs, cubed	½ cup chicken stock	Grated zest of 1 orange
¼ teaspoon garlic powder	1 tablespoon vegetable oil	½ cup packed brown sugar	8 ounces sugar snap peas
¼ teaspoon ground ginger	¾ cup freshly squeezed orange juice, divided	3 tablespoons soy sauce	Steamed rice, for serving (optional)
		1½ tablespoons rice vinegar	Red pepper flakes, for spice (optional)

1. Mix 2 tablespoons of cornstarch, the garlic powder, and ground ginger in a small bowl. Toss the chicken in the cornstarch mixture until evenly coated.

2. Select the Sauté function. Heat the oil in the inner pot. Add the chicken and sauté for 5 minutes, stirring occasionally. Transfer the chicken from the pot to a plate and set aside. Press Cancel.

3. Pour ½ cup of orange juice, the stock, sugar, soy sauce, vinegar, and orange zest into the pot and stir with a wooden spoon, scraping the bottom of the pot to loosen any brown bits. Return the chicken to the pot and stir.

4. Close the lid and set the cooking time to 6 minutes at high/normal pressure. It will take 8 minutes to reach pressure.

5. Quick release the pressure. Whisk the remaining 2 tablespoons of cornstarch with the remaining ¼ cup of orange juice. Open the lid and select the Sauté function again.

6. Stir the cornstarch mixture into the pot, then add the snap peas. Cook for 3 minutes. Press Cancel and serve with rice and red pepper flakes (if using).

Per serving: Calories: 285; Fat: 7g; Protein: 24g; Carbohydrates: 30g; Fiber: 1g; Sugar: 22g; Sodium: 555mg

Cottage Pie

Page 104

Chapter 7

Beef & Pork

95

SICHUAN-INSPIRED BEEF

› SERVES 4
› **Prep time:** 5 minutes
› **Sauté:** 6 minutes

› **Pressure cook:** 10 minutes High
› **Pressure Release:** Quick
› **Total time:** 30 Minutes

Chinese takeout is one of my all-time favorite comfort foods. When I can make takeout-style recipes myself at home with little effort, it's a win-win. Cooked in the Instant Pot, this delicious and spicy beef dish comes out incredibly tender and makes lip-smacking leftovers for lunch the next day (that is, if there are any leftovers!).

2 tablespoons sesame oil

1½ pounds flank steak, cut into thin strips

2 garlic cloves, minced

¾ teaspoon grated fresh ginger

¼ cup hoisin sauce

¼ cup soy sauce

1 tablespoon brown sugar

1 tablespoon sriracha sauce

1 teaspoon rice vinegar

¼ teaspoon red pepper flakes

½ cup beef stock

2 tablespoons water

2 tablespoons cornstarch

1 cup julienned celery

½ cup julienned carrots

¼ cup chopped scallions, green parts only

Steamed rice, for serving (optional)

1. Select the Sauté function. Heat the oil in the inner pot. Add the steak to the pot and sauté for 3 to 4 minutes until the steak is just starting to brown. Add the garlic and ginger to the pot and stir to combine. Sauté for 1 minute more. Press Cancel.

2. In a medium bowl, whisk together the hoisin sauce, soy sauce, brown sugar, sriracha, vinegar, and red pepper flakes.

3. Add the stock to the pot and stir with a wooden spoon, scraping the bottom of the pot to loosen any brown bits. Pour the soy sauce mixture over everything and stir to combine.

4. Close the lid and set the cooking time to 10 minutes at high/normal pressure. It will take 6 minutes to reach pressure.

5. Quick release the pressure. Open the lid. In a small bowl, whisk together the water and cornstarch.

6. Select the Sauté function again. Add the cornstarch mixture, celery, and carrots to the pot. Simmer for about 1 minute until the sauce thickens and the vegetables are crisp-tender. Press Cancel.

7. Top with the scallions and serve with rice (if using).

8. Store leftovers in an airtight container in the refrigerator.

Flavor Boost

If you like your food with some heat, you can make this meal even spicier by adding up to 2 more tablespoons of sriracha and ¼ teaspoon more red pepper flakes. If, however, you prefer a less spicy meal, dial down the heat by omitting the sriracha and using just a pinch of red pepper flakes.

Per serving: Calories: 423; Fat: 22g; Protein: 38g; Carbohydrates: 17g; Fiber: 2g; Sugar: 8g; Sodium: 1,158mg

SPICY BROCCOLI BEEF

> SERVES 4
> **Prep time:** 8 minutes
> **Sauté:** 12 minutes

> **Pressure cook:** 1 minute Low
> **Release:** Quick
> **Total time:** 30 minutes

In this recipe, searing a whole sirloin steak provides the flavor that comes from stir-frying over high heat, but without the risk of overcooking. And because the meat cooks quickly, it can go in the pot with the broccoli and cook at the same time.

- 3 tablespoons vegetable oil, divided
- 2 (12- to 14-ounce) top sirloin steaks, about 1 inch thick
- ½ teaspoon kosher salt
- ¼ cup dry sherry
- ½ cup beef stock
- ¼ cup water
- 12 ounces broccoli florets (2 medium crowns)
- 1 red bell pepper, seeded and sliced
- ¼ cup soy sauce
- 2 tablespoons oyster sauce
- 2 tablespoons rice vinegar
- 2 tablespoons orange juice concentrate
- 1 tablespoon chili garlic sauce, or more as desired
- 2 teaspoons cornstarch
- 1 tablespoon minced peeled fresh ginger
- 1 tablespoon minced garlic
- 2 scallions, sliced, white and green parts separated
- Steamed rice, for serving

1. Select the Sauté function. Heat 2 tablespoons of oil in the inner pot. Sprinkle both sides of the steak with the salt. Lay the beef in a single layer in the pot without crowding (work in batches if necessary). Sear the beef for 1½ minutes. Flip the steaks and cook on the other side for a further 1½ minutes. Transfer the beef to a rack or plate.

2. Pour the oil out of the pot and add the sherry. Bring it to a simmer and cook for 2 to 3 minutes, scraping the bottom of the pan with a wooden spoon to loosen any brown bits, until the sherry has reduced by about half. Add the stock and water to the pot. Press Cancel.

3. Place a steamer rack trivet in the bottom of the pot. Arrange the broccoli and bell pepper in a steamer basket and place the steaks on top of the vegetables. Place the basket on the trivet.

4. Close the lid and set the cooking time to 1 minute at low pressure. It will take 6 minutes to reach pressure.

5. Quick release the pressure. Open the lid and remove the steamer basket of broccoli and bell pepper and the trivet and set aside. Transfer the steaks to a plate or cutting board.

6. Pour the beef broth mixture from the pot into a small bowl. Add the soy sauce, oyster sauce, vinegar, orange juice concentrate, chili garlic sauce, and cornstarch and whisk together. Set aside.

7. Select the Sauté function again. Heat the remaining 1 tablespoon of oil in the pot. Add the ginger, garlic, and the white parts of the scallions and cook for about 2 minutes, stirring frequently, until fragrant. Add the reserved beef broth mixture. Stir to combine and cook for 2 to 3 minutes, stirring occasionally, until the sauce has thickened. Adjust the heat to low heat.

8. While the sauce cooks, slice the steaks about ⅛ inch thick. If the slices are large, cut them into bite-size pieces. The steak might be raw in the center. Don't worry; it will cook again. Add the beef slices, broccoli, and bell pepper to the sauce in the pot and stir to coat. Cook just long enough for the beef to finish cooking and the vegetables to warm through. (If the beef is quite raw in the center, let it cook first for a minute or so, then add the vegetables). Press Cancel.

9. Serve with rice and garnish with the green parts of the scallions.

10. Store leftovers in an airtight container in the refrigerator.

Substitution Tip

If you prefer not to serve this with rice, you can skip the extra starch and add more veggies such as yellow squash, zucchini, and celery along with the broccoli, using the same cooking time.

Per serving: Calories: 507; Fat: 30g; Protein: 40g; Carbohydrates: 15g; Fiber: 3g; Sugar: 5g; Sodium: 1,215mg

BEEF STROGANOFF

> SERVES 4
> **Prep time:** 5 minutes
> **Sauté:** 8 minutes

> **Pressure cook:** 5 minutes High
> **Release:** Quick
> **Total time:** 30 minutes

Beef stroganoff reminds me of my childhood, and now I love seeing my own children dig into the creamy, beefy sauce when I make it. Serve it with buttered egg noodles for a wonderfully satisfying meal.

1 tablespoon vegetable oil	1 medium onion, halved and sliced	¼ teaspoon freshly ground black pepper	½ cup sour cream
6 ounces sliced steak for stir-fry	1 cup beef stock	¼ teaspoon garlic powder	¼ teaspoon dried dill
8 ounces sliced mushrooms	½ teaspoon salt	1 tablespoon cornstarch	¼ cup chopped scallions, green parts only

1. Select the Sauté function. Heat the oil in the inner pot. Add the steak, mushrooms, and onion to the pot and sauté for about 5 minutes until the steak is just starting to brown and the mushrooms are starting to soften. Press Cancel.

2. Add the stock, salt, pepper, and garlic powder to the pot and stir with a wooden spoon, scraping the bottom of the pot to loosen any brown bits.

3. Close the lid and set the cooking time to 5 minutes at high/normal pressure. It will take 6 minutes to reach pressure.

4. Quick release the pressure. Open the lid. In a small bowl, whisk 1 tablespoon of the sauce from the pot with the cornstarch.

5. Select the Sauté function again. Add the cornstarch mixture, sour cream, and dill to the pot. Sauté for about 3 minutes, stirring, until the sour cream has blended into the sauce and the sauce has thickened. Press Cancel and top with scallions. Store leftovers in an airtight container in the refrigerator.

Flavor Boost

Add 2 tablespoons Worcestershire sauce to the beef stock.

Per serving: Calories: 201; Fat: 14g; Protein: 12g; Carbohydrates: 8g; Fiber: 1g; Sugar: 3g; Sodium: 332mg

CHEESEBURGER MACARONI

› SERVES 6
› **Prep time:** 3 minutes
› **Sauté:** 6 minutes
› **Pressure cook:** 6 minutes High

› **Release:** Quick
› **Total time:** 30 minutes
› One-Pot Meal

This homemade cheeseburger mac is just as easy to whip up as the boxed stuff, but it's more than twice as good. It could serve up to eight people, but if your family is anything like mine, they will want seconds.

1 pound ground beef
4 cups beef stock
2 teaspoons paprika
1 teaspoon salt

½ teaspoon garlic powder
½ teaspoon onion powder

¼ teaspoon freshly ground black pepper
16 ounces dried elbow macaroni

¾ cup milk
3 cups shredded cheddar cheese

1. Select the Sauté function. Place the beef in the pot and sauté for 6 minutes, stirring occasionally. While the beef cooks, prep the remaining ingredients. Press Cancel and transfer the beef to a plate. Set aside.

2. Pour the stock, paprika, salt, garlic powder, onion powder, and pepper into the pot and stir, scraping the bottom of the pot with a wooden spoon to loosen any brown bits.

3. Add the macaroni to the pot, making sure the noodles are mostly submerged in the liquid, but do not stir. Lay the reserved beef on top of the pasta.

4. Close the lid and set the cooking time to 6 minutes at high/normal pressure. It will take 12 minutes to reach pressure.

5. Quick release the pressure. Open the lid and gradually stir in the milk and cheddar cheese, alternating between a little of the milk and a handful of cheese at a time, and stir until the cheese is melted and the sauce has thickened.

6. Store leftovers in an airtight container in the refrigerator.

Variation Tip

Try substituting 1 cup of Monterey Jack for 1 cup of cheddar cheese.

Per serving: Calories: 665; Fat: 29g; Protein: 40g; Carbohydrates: 59g; Fiber: 3g; Sugar: 4g; Sodium: 820mg

GREEN CURRY PORK

> SERVES 4
> **Prep time:** 5 minutes
> **Pressure cook:** 4 minutes High
> **Sauté:** 4 minutes

> **Release:** Quick
> **Total time:** 20 minutes
> One-Pot Meal, Super Quick

There's nothing quite like curry to warm you up on a cold winter night. Green chiles, lemongrass, and lime peel give green curry a bright, citrusy flavor that's less fiery than red curries. If this dish is still too spicy for your taste, you can tone it down by stirring a tablespoon of your favorite sweetener into the pot. Serve with brown or white rice, if desired.

1 (13.5-ounce) can full-fat unsweetened coconut milk	¼ cup green curry paste	4 carrots, cut into coins	1 tablespoon maple syrup or coconut sugar (optional)
⅓ cup water	1 pound pork tenderloin, thinly sliced	⅔ pound fresh green beans, trimmed	Cilantro, for garnish (optional)

1. Pour the coconut milk, water, and curry paste into the inner pot and mix together until smooth. Add the pork. (There's no need to mix the pork with the sauce.)

2. Close the lid and set the cooking time to 4 minutes at high/normal pressure. It will take 6 minutes to reach pressure.

3. Quick release the pressure. Open the lid and select the Sauté function. Add the carrots and green beans and simmer, uncovered, for 4 minutes or until the vegetables are tender. Press Cancel. Taste the curry and stir in the maple syrup (if using) before serving. Garnish with cilantro (if using).

4. Store leftovers in an airtight container in the refrigerator.

Substitution Tip

For a vegan version of this curry, swap the pork for a large diced sweet potato and add 2 cups of fresh broccoli florets with the other vegetables. The cook time remains the same.

Per serving: Calories: 381; Fat: 24g; Protein: 29g; Carbohydrates: 17g; Fiber: 7g; Sugar: 5g; Sodium: 122mg

COTTAGE PIE

› SERVES 6
› **Prep time:** 5 minutes
› **Sauté:** 7 minutes
› **Pressure cook:** 7 minutes High

› **Release:** Quick
› **Total time:** 30 minutes
› One-Pot Meal

This is one of those meals that highlights just how versatile Instant Pots can be. Ground beef and vegetables sauté together before you make mashed potatoes in the same pot. In just 30 minutes, you have the meat, vegetables, and potatoes ready to go and combined into a delicious comfort food that your family will request again and again.

1 pound ground beef
1 cup diced onion
3 garlic cloves, minced
½ teaspoon salt
¼ teaspoon freshly ground black pepper

1 (15-ounce) can peas and carrots, drained
¼ cup beef stock
2 tablespoons Worcestershire sauce
1 tablespoon tomato paste

½ teaspoon dried thyme
1 cup water
3 medium potatoes, peeled and chopped into 1-inch cubes

1 cup shredded sharp cheddar cheese, divided
½ cup half-and-half
2 tablespoons butter
¼ teaspoon garlic salt

1. Select the Sauté function. Combine the beef, onion, garlic, salt, and pepper in the inner pot and sauté for 6 minutes, stirring occasionally, until the onion is soft.

2. While the beef cooks, prep the remaining ingredients.

3. Stir the peas and carrots, stock, Worcestershire sauce, tomato paste, and thyme into the beef mixture. Sauté for 1 more minute. Press Cancel and transfer the beef mixture to an 8-inch square baking pan. Clean out the pot.

4. Pour the water into the pot and place a steamer rack trivet in the bottom.

5. Arrange the potatoes in a steamer basket. Place the basket on the trivet.

6. Close the lid and set the cooking time to 7 minutes at high/normal pressure. It will take 6 minutes to reach pressure.

7. Quick release the pressure. Open the lid and transfer the potatoes to a large bowl.

8. Add ¾ cup of cheddar cheese, the half-and-half, butter, and garlic salt to the potatoes. Mash until well blended. Spread the mashed potatoes evenly over the beef mixture in the baking pan. Sprinkle the remaining ¼ cup of cheddar cheese on top of the mashed potatoes.

9. Preheat a broiler and place the cottage pie under the heat source for 3 minutes or until the top starts to turn golden.

10. To store, cover the pan with aluminum foil and refrigerate. To reheat, you can microwave individual portions, or heat the entire baking pan in the oven at 350°F until warmed through.

Substitution Tip

Want to make this a more traditional shepherd's pie? Substitute ground lamb for the ground beef.

Per serving: Calories: 417; Fat: 20g; Protein: 26g; Carbohydrates: 33g; Fiber: 6g; Sugar: 7g; Sodium: 471mg

PORK CHOPS WITH APPLES AND ONIONS

› SERVES 4

› **Prep time:** 3 minutes

› **Sauté:** 5 minutes

› **Pressure cook:** 3 minutes High

› **Release:** Natural for 7 minutes, then Quick Release

› **Total time:** 30 minutes

› One-Pot Meal

This warm and hearty dinner is perfect for the fall. Boneless pork chops and onions are pressure cooked in apple cider and chicken stock, and finished with cream and sliced apples. It creates a fragrant dish that is sure to become a family favorite.

2 tablespoons vegetable oil	Freshly ground black pepper	½ cup chicken stock	1 tablespoon cornstarch
4 boneless pork chops	1 medium onion, sliced	¾ teaspoon dried thyme	2 medium apples, cored and sliced
Pinch salt, plus ½ teaspoon	1 cup apple cider	¼ cup heavy (whipping) cream	

1. Select the Sauté function. Heat the oil in the inner pot.

2. Season both sides of the pork chops with a pinch of salt and some pepper, then place them in the pot. Spread the onion around the pork. Sauté the pork for 2 minutes per side and occasionally stir the onion. Press Cancel.

3. Pour the apple cider, stock, thyme, and the remaining ½ teaspoon of salt into the pot and stir, scraping the bottom of the pot with a wooden spoon to loosen any brown bits.

4. Close the lid and set the cooking time to 3 minutes at high/normal pressure. It will take 12 minutes to reach pressure.

5. Allow the pressure to release from the pot naturally for 7 minutes, then quick release the remaining pressure. While the pressure is releasing, whisk the cream and cornstarch together in a small bowl.

6. Open the lid and select the Sauté function again. Stir the cornstarch mixture and apples into the pot and simmer for about 1 minute until the sauce thickens. Press Cancel. The apples will soften in the hot sauce.

7. Store leftovers in an airtight container in the refrigerator.'

Substitution Tip

Try this recipe with bone-in chicken thighs instead of pork. Increase the pressure-cooking time to 10 minutes with a 10-minute natural release.

Per serving: Calories: 382; Fat: 20g; Protein: 25g; Carbohydrates: 24g; Fiber: 3g; Sugar: 17g; Sodium: 394mg

SMOTHERED PORK CHOPS

› SERVES 4
› **Prep time:** 5 minutes
› **Sauté:** 15 minutes
› **Pressure cook:** 1 minute Low

› **Release:** Natural for 4 minutes, then Quick Release
› **Total time:** 30 minutes
› One-Pot Meal

Pork loin chops need very little time in the Instant Pot before they become overcooked. But with a little care, you can turn out beautifully brown, tender chops—and make a creamy, delicious sauce at the same time. This is a great meal to serve for a stay-at-home date night or when you have guests. This is lovely garnished with fresh thyme.

2 tablespoons vegetable oil

4 boneless pork loin chops

1½ teaspoons kosher salt, divided, plus more as needed

1½ cups thinly sliced onion

8 ounces sliced white button or cremini mushrooms

½ teaspoon dried thyme

¼ teaspoon freshly ground black pepper, plus more as needed

½ cup dry white wine

1 cup chicken stock

2 teaspoons Worcestershire sauce

1 tablespoon all-purpose flour

2 tablespoons sour cream

1. Select the Sauté function. Heat the oil in the inner pot. Season both sides of the pork with 1 teaspoon of salt, then place the chops in the pot. Let them cook, undisturbed, for about 3 minutes or until golden brown. Flip the chops and brown the other side for 3 minutes. Transfer the chops to a plate.

2. Add the onion to the pot and cook for 2 minutes, stirring frequently, until the onion pieces start to separate and soften. Add the mushrooms and sprinkle with the remaining ½ teaspoon of salt, the thyme, and pepper. Cook for 2 minutes, stirring occasionally, until the mushrooms are soft and starting to brown.

3. Add the wine and scrape the bottom of the pot with a wooden spoon to loosen any brown bits. Let the wine simmer for 3 minutes until reduced by about half.

4. In a medium bowl, whisk together the stock, Worcestershire sauce, and flour. Add to the pot and stir to combine with the onion and mushrooms. Press Cancel and return the pork to the pot. Spoon some of the onion mixture over the pork.

5. Close the lid and set the cooking time to 1 minute at low pressure. It will take 7 minutes to reach pressure.

CONTINUED →

6. Allow the pressure to release from the pot naturally for 4 minutes, then quick release the remaining pressure.

7. Open the lid and transfer the pork chops to a serving platter. Add the sour cream to the sauce and stir to combine. Taste and adjust the seasoning, adding more salt or pepper if necessary. Spoon the sauce over the chops and serve.

8. Store leftovers in an airtight container in the refrigerator.

Flavor Boost

To up the decadence in this one-pot dinner, substitute heavy (whipping) cream for the sour cream.

Per serving: Calories: 336; Fat: 13g; Protein: 40g; Carbohydrates: 8g; Fiber: 1g; Sugar: 4g; Sodium: 1,180mg

PORK TENDERLOIN WITH CABBAGE AND NOODLES

> SERVES 4
> **Prep time:** 5 minutes
> **Sauté:** 14 minutes
> **Pressure cook:** 4 minutes Low

> **Release:** Quick
> **Total time:** 30 minutes
> One-Pot Meal

The beauty of cooking a pork tenderloin in an Instant Pot is that it cooks so quickly you can pair it with noodles or vegetables—they'll be done in the same length of time. The classic German or Eastern European dish of cabbage and noodles makes a tasty and filling accompaniment.

3 bacon
  slices, chopped
1 (1¼-pound) pork
  tenderloin, halved
  crosswise

1 teaspoon kosher
  salt, plus more as
  necessary
¼ teaspoon freshly
  ground black
  pepper, plus more as
  necessary

1 teaspoon smoked or
  regular paprika
1 cup sliced onion
½ very small head
  green cabbage,
  shredded

⅓ cup dry white wine
1¼ cups chicken
  stock, plus more as
  necessary
4 ounces wide
  egg noodles

1. Select the Sauté function. Put the bacon in the inner pot and cook for about 6 minutes until most of the fat has rendered and the bacon is crisp. Use a slotted spoon to transfer the bacon to a paper towel–lined plate, leaving the rendered fat in the pot.

2. Sprinkle the tenderloin halves with the salt, pepper, and paprika.

3. Add the pork to the pot and sear, undisturbed, for 2 to 3 minutes until brown, then turn and sear the other side. Transfer to a plate.

4. Add the onion and cabbage to the pot and stir to coat with the remaining fat. Cook for about 2 minutes, stirring frequently, or until the vegetables start to soften. Add the wine and bring to a simmer, scraping the bottom of the pot with a wooden spoon to loosen any brown bits. Let the wine reduce slightly. Press Cancel.

5. Add the stock and noodles and stir to cover the noodles with the liquid (add more stock if the noodles are not fully submerged). Place the pork tenderloin halves on top of the vegetables and noodles.

CONTINUED →

6. Close the lid and set the cooking time to 4 minutes at low pressure. It will take 7 minutes to reach pressure.

7. Quick release the pressure. Open the lid and check the temperature of the pork; it should be about 145°F. If it is much lower than that, put it back with the noodles and put the lid on, but don't lock it into place. Check it again after a couple of minutes.

8. Once the pork is done, transfer it to a cutting board and let it rest for a couple of minutes. Taste the noodles and cabbage and adjust the seasoning, adding more salt and pepper if necessary, then spoon into a serving dish. Slice the pork and serve with the cabbage and noodles.

9. Store leftovers in an airtight container in the refrigerator.

Substitution Tip

If you don't have white wine or prefer not to cook with it, you can substitute an additional ⅓ cup of chicken stock for the wine.

Per serving: Calories: 406; Fat: 15g; Protein: 48g; Carbohydrates: 15g; Fiber: 3g; Sugar: 5g; Sodium: 1,699mg

TUSCAN-INSPIRED SAUSAGE FETTUCCINE

> SERVES 6
> **Prep time:** 7 minutes
> **Pressure cook:** 6 minutes High

> **Release:** Quick
> **Total time:** 30 minutes
> One-Pot Meal

One-pot pastas are my favorite busy weeknight dinner solution. Not only does my family love creamy, cheesy pastas like this dish, but I also love how hands-off the preparation is, which allows me to multitask while dinner cooks.

- 3 cups chicken stock
- 1 tablespoon freshly squeezed lemon juice
- 1 teaspoon dried basil
- ½ teaspoon salt
- ½ teaspoon freshly ground black pepper
- ½ teaspoon garlic powder
- 12 ounces dried fettuccine pasta, broken in half
- 10 ounces cooked Italian sausage crumbles
- 1 (8-ounce) package cream cheese, cubed
- ⅓ cup oil-packed sun-dried tomatoes, drained
- ½ cup shredded parmesan cheese, plus more as desired
- 2 cups baby spinach

1. Pour the stock, lemon juice, basil, salt, pepper, and garlic powder into the inner pot and stir. Add the fettuccine, making sure the noodles are all submerged, but do not stir.

2. Place the sausage on top of the noodles, followed by the cream cheese and tomatoes.

3. Close the lid and set the cooking time to 6 minutes at high/normal pressure for al dente pasta (add 1 minute if you want softer noodles). It will take 12 minutes to reach pressure.

4. Quick release the pressure. Open the lid and add the parmesan cheese to the pot, stirring until the cheese has completely blended into the pasta sauce and any noodles that were stuck together have broken up. Stir in the spinach and let the pasta sit in the pot, stirring it occasionally, for 2 minutes. Serve in bowls, garnished with additional parmesan cheese, if desired.

5. Store leftovers in an airtight container in the refrigerator.

Flavor Boost

Garnish it with fresh basil, red pepper flakes, and additional parmesan cheese.

Per serving: Calories: 539; Fat: 29g; Protein: 22g; Carbohydrates: 50g; Fiber: 3g; Sugar: 4g; Sodium: 1,071mg

Mini Funfetti Cupcakes

Page 116

Chapter 8

Dessert

MINI FUNFETTI CUPCAKES

> MAKES 7 CUPCAKES
> **Prep time:** 5 minutes
> **Pressure cook:** 12 minutes High

> **Release:** Natural for 5 minutes, then Quick Release
> **Total time:** 30 minutes

Many people are surprised to learn that you can make fluffy "baked goods" in your Instant Pot. Because they are technically steamed in a high-pressure environment, rather than being baked, the results are moist and full of flavor. These mini cupcakes are one of my kids' favorite Instant Pot recipes.

1 cup water	¼ cup plain, nonfat Greek yogurt	⅓ cup sugar	4 tablespoons rainbow sprinkles, divided
Nonstick cooking spray	1 large egg	½ teaspoon baking powder	½ cup buttercream frosting
¼ cup unsalted butter, at room temperature	¾ cup all-purpose flour, spooned and leveled	½ teaspoon baking soda	
		Pinch salt	

1. Pour the water into the inner pot and place a steamer rack trivet in the bottom.

2. Spray the cups of a silicone egg bite mold with cooking spray.

3. In a small bowl, beat the butter, yogurt, and egg together with a hand mixer until smooth. In a medium bowl, stir together the flour, sugar, baking powder, baking soda, and salt. Add the wet ingredients to the dry ingredients and beat with the hand mixer until well combined (the batter will be thick). Stir in 3 tablespoons of sprinkles.

4. Divide the batter evenly among the seven cups of the egg bite mold, then shake the mold so the batter settles into each cup. Lay a paper towel over the top of the mold (this helps catch excess moisture from the steam inside the pot), then cover the paper towel and egg bite mold loosely with aluminum foil. Place the egg bite mold on the trivet.

5. Close the lid and set the cooking time to 12 minutes at high/normal pressure. It will take 6 minutes to reach pressure.

6. Allow the pressure to release from the pot naturally for 5 minutes, then quick release the remaining pressure. Use a butter knife to remove the mini cupcakes from the mold. Allow to cool on a wire rack for 2 minutes. Frost the tops of the cupcakes with buttercream frosting and sprinkle with the remaining 1 tablespoon of rainbow sprinkles.

7. Store leftovers in an airtight container at room temperature for up to 2 days.

Flavor Boost

Add a splash of vanilla extract to the batter for an extra boost of flavor—just a splash because the alcohol can't cook off in the pressurized environment. (Steam doesn't escape while it cooks.)

Per serving (1 cupcake): Calories: 270; Fat: 12g; Protein: 3g; Carbohydrates: 37g; Fiber: 1g; Sugar: 26g; Sodium: 200mg

SPICED POACHED PEARS

> SERVES 4
> **Prep time:** 5 minutes
> **Sauté:** 10 minutes
> **Pressure cook:** 6 minutes High

> **Release:** Quick
> **Total time:** 30 minutes
> 5-Ingredient

This light dessert is ready to serve in a snap and couldn't be easier. Poaching pears in an Instant Pot saves at least half the amount of time of poaching them on the stovetop, and is also less complicated. These pears are fabulous on their own, or try them with a dollop of ice cream or whipped cream.

5 to 6 cups apple cider   2 cinnamon sticks   1 teaspoon   4 pears
2 tablespoons honey   whole cloves

1. Select the Sauté function. Combine the apple cider, honey, cinnamon sticks, and cloves in the inner pot and stir together. Simmer for about 10 minutes until the liquid reaches a boil. Press Cancel.

2. While the juice is simmering, peel the skin off the pears, leaving the stems on. Slice the bottoms off the pears (so they have a flat surface to stand up in serving bowls later).

3. Lay the pears on their sides in the pot. (There should be enough liquid to mostly submerge the pears; if not, add some additional apple cider.) Close the lid and set the cooking time to 6 minutes at high/normal pressure. It will take 8 to 9 minutes to reach pressure.

4. Quick release the pressure. Open the lid.

5. Using tongs, carefully remove the pears by their stems, so the tongs don't puncture the soft fruit. Place one pear in each in four serving bowls. Pour up to 1 cup of liquid from the pot into each bowl and serve hot.

Flavor Boost

These are wonderful on their own, but you can up the decadence factor by drizzling caramel over the pears when serving.

Per serving: Calories: 276; Fat: 1g; Protein: 1g; Carbohydrates: 71g; Fiber: 6g; Sugar: 56g; Sodium: 15mg

BLACKBERRY CRISP

› SERVES 4
› **Prep time:** 5 minutes
› **Pressure cook:** 10 minutes High

› **Release:** Natural for 5 minutes, then Quick Release
› **Total time:** 30 minutes

This dessert is on repeat at our house. It's so easy to make, and so, so good. We love to serve it with a scoop of vanilla ice cream, whipped cream, or yogurt.

1 cup water

Nonstick cooking spray

2 (6-ounce) packages fresh blackberries

3 tablespoons sugar

1 teaspoon freshly squeezed lemon juice

1 cup old-fashioned oats

⅓ cup all-purpose flour

½ cup packed brown sugar

½ teaspoon ground cinnamon

¼ teaspoon ground nutmeg

Pinch salt

½ cup unsalted butter, melted

1. Pour the water into the inner pot and place a steamer rack trivet in the bottom.

2. Spray a 7-inch wide heat-safe glass bowl or round baking pan with cooking spray. In a separate bowl, mix the blackberries, sugar, and lemon juice. In a third bowl, stir together the oats, flour, brown sugar, cinnamon, nutmeg, and salt. Add the butter and stir until well mixed and crumbly.

3. Pour the blackberry mixture into the prepared heat-safe bowl. Top evenly with the crumble mixture. Cover the bowl with aluminum foil, then place the bowl on the trivet in the pot.

4. Close the lid and set the cooking time to 10 minutes at high/normal pressure. It will take 7 minutes to reach pressure.

5. Allow the pressure to release from the pot naturally for 5 minutes, then quick release the remaining pressure. Remove the bowl from the pot and remove the foil. Place the bowl under a broiler for about 3 minutes, until the top is crisped. Serve in bowls.

6. Store leftovers in an airtight container in the refrigerator.

Variation Tip

Use blueberries, raspberries, or strawberries instead of blackberries.

Per serving: Calories: 529; Fat: 25g; Protein: 6g; Carbohydrates: 74g; Fiber: 7g; Sugar: 45g; Sodium: 51mg

EASY S'MORES DIP

› SERVES 4
› **Prep time:** 3 minutes
› **Pressure cook:** 4 minutes High

› **Release:** Quick
› **Total time:** 15 minutes
› 5-Ingredient, Super Quick

This kid-friendly treat can be whipped up so quickly and easily that it works equally well for a dessert or an after-school snack. It's delicious with milk chocolate or dark chocolate chips. For more of a campfire-inspired feel, place the ramekins under a broiler briefly after pressure cooking.

1 cup water
½ cup chocolate chips, divided

¾ cup mini marshmallows, divided

4 graham crackers, each broken into 4 segments

1. Pour the water into the inner pot and place a steamer rack trivet in the bottom.

2. Put 2 tablespoons of chocolate chips in each of four (4½-ounce) ramekins. Add 3 tablespoons of mini marshmallows on top of the chocolate chips in each ramekin. Place the ramekins on the trivet.

3. Close the lid and set the cooking time to 4 minutes at high/normal pressure. It will take 6 minutes to reach pressure.

4. Quick release the pressure.

5. Open the lid and carefully remove the ramekins. Serve warm, each with 4 graham cracker segments.

Variation Tip

Instead of individual portions, you can make this a larger, party-size portion by layering the ingredients into a larger heat-safe dish and pressure cooking for 5 minutes instead of 4 minutes.

Per serving: Calories: 213; Fat: 10g; Protein: 2g; Carbohydrates: 30g; Fiber: 2g; Sugar: 17g; Sodium: 74mg

ARROZ CON DULCE (PUERTO RICAN-STYLE RICE PUDDING)

> SERVES 6

> **Prep time:** 4 minutes
> **Sauté:** 5 minutes
> **Pressure cook:** 7 minutes High

> **Release:** Natural for 5 minutes, then Quick Release
> **Total time:** 30 minutes

Arroz con dulce, which means "rice with candy," is a sweet rice pudding that's popular in Puerto Rico during the holidays. Each family has its own way of making it, so feel free to experiment with the spices and flavors to make this one your own.

1 (13.5-ounce) can coconut milk

1 cup water

2 cinnamon sticks

6 whole cloves

½ teaspoon ground ginger

¼ teaspoon ground nutmeg

¼ teaspoon salt

1 cup arborio rice

½ cup sugar

½ cup raisins

Ground cinnamon, for garnish

1. Select the Sauté function. Combine the coconut milk, water, cinnamon sticks, cloves, ginger, nutmeg, and salt in the inner pot and stir. Sauté, stirring occasionally, for 5 minutes. Press Cancel. Remove and discard the cinnamon sticks and cloves.

2. Stir the rice and sugar into the spiced coconut milk.

3. Close the lid and set the cooking time to 7 minutes at high/normal pressure. It will take 5 minutes to reach pressure.

4. Allow the pressure to release from the pot naturally for 5 minutes, then quick release the remaining pressure. Open the lid and stir in the raisins. Let the rice sit in the pot, uncovered, for 3 minutes to thicken. Serve sprinkled with cinnamon.

5. Although best served hot, leftovers can be stored in an airtight container in the refrigerator.

Variation Tip

Swap the raisins for dried cranberries, or skip them altogether.

Per serving: Calories: 346; Fat: 14g; Protein: 4g; Carbohydrates: 55g; Fiber: 1g; Sugar: 25g; Sodium: 109mg

CHOCOLATE CHIP MUG COOKIES

> SERVES 1
> **Prep time:** 5 minutes
> **Pressure cook:** 10 minutes High

> **Release:** Natural for 5 minutes, then Quick Release
> **Total time:** 30 minutes

This recipe is great for satisfying a dessert craving for a single serving, or you can make a few at a time if you're serving more than one person. Scale the recipe and use individual jars for each portion. You can make as many servings as you can fit jars on the trivet; the cooking time remains the same.

1 cup water
1 tablespoon unsalted butter, melted
1 large egg yolk

1 tablespoon granulated sugar
1 tablespoon dark brown sugar

2 tablespoons all-purpose flour
Pinch salt

1 tablespoon semisweet chocolate chips

1. Pour the water into the inner pot and place a steamer rack trivet in the bottom.

2. In an 8-ounce mason jar, whisk together the butter, egg yolk, granulated sugar, and brown sugar. Add the flour and salt to the jar and stir until well combined. Stir the chocolate chips into the jar, then cover with aluminum foil. Place the jar on the trivet.

3. Close the lid and set the cooking time to 10 minutes at high/normal pressure (8 minutes for gooier cookies). It will take 6 minutes to reach pressure.

4. Allow the pressure to release from the pot naturally for 5 minutes, then quick release the remaining pressure.

5. Open the lid and carefully remove the jar. Allow to cool on a wire rack for 2 to 3 minutes before eating.

Substitution Tip

You can make these gluten-free by swapping almond flour for the all-purpose flour. This will yield a much gooier cookie, so I recommend using the longer cooking time.

Per serving: Calories: 354; Fat: 20g; Protein: 5g; Carbohydrates: 39g; Fiber: 1g; Sugar: 25g; Sodium: 258mg

CHOCOLATE-DIPPED STRAWBERRIES

> › SERVES 9
> › **Prep time:** 2 minutes
> › **Sauté:** 7 minutes

> › **Total time:** 25 minutes
> › 5-Ingredient

Although most people are aware of the Instant Pot's pressure cook, sauté, and steam functions, many are surprised to learn that this truly multifunctional device also makes an effective double boiler that's perfect for melting chocolate.

2 cups water	1 (12-ounce) pack semisweet chocolate chips	1 tablespoon coconut oil	36 large strawberries

1. Line a baking sheet or cutting board with wax paper.

2. Pour the water into the inner pot. Select the Sauté function and bring the water to a simmer.

3. In a heat-safe glass or stainless-steel bowl that fits on the top of the inner pot (with a base that is small enough to fit inside the pot, but with a top that is wide enough that it rests on the pot rim), stir together the chocolate chips and coconut oil. Place the bowl on the pot.

4. Cook over the simmering water for 7 minutes or until the chips are completely melted, stirring constantly. Carefully remove the bowl from the pot and press Cancel.

5. Dip the strawberries into the melted chocolate, then place them on the prepared baking sheet. Place the baking sheet in the refrigerator for 15 minutes or until the chocolate coating hardens. A freezer will expedite the process.

6. Store leftovers in an airtight container in the refrigerator.

Variation Tip

Use this same method with white chocolate. You can also add sprinkles, nuts, or candy melt stripes on top of the berries before the chocolate hardens.

Per serving: Calories: 255; Fat: 16g; Protein: 3g; Carbohydrates: 25g; Fiber: 5g; Sugar: 17g; Sodium: 5mg

Hot Pepper Sauce

Page 129

Chapter 9

Staples

SMOKY BARBECUE SAUCE

> MAKES 2 CUPS
> **Prep time:** 8 minutes
> **Pressure cook:** 8 minutes High

> **Release:** Natural for 5 minutes, then Quick Release
> **Total time:** 30 minutes

If you find commercial barbecue sauces too sweet for your taste, this sauce is for you. It has an undertone of ancho chile and smoke from the paprika and chipotle. It's a bit spicy, but it has a good balance of acid and sugar.

1 dried ancho chile, stemmed and seeded

1 small onion, cut into eighths

2 garlic cloves, lightly smashed

1½ cups drained tomatoes, or tomato sauce

2 tablespoons unsalted butter

1 tablespoon apple cider vinegar

1 tablespoon molasses

1 teaspoon chipotle puree

1 teaspoon Worcestershire sauce

2 tablespoons brown sugar

1 teaspoon smoked paprika

1 teaspoon mustard powder

1 teaspoon kosher salt

½ teaspoon freshly ground black pepper

1. Put the chile in the inner pot, then thoroughly wash your hands to avoid getting any chile in your eyes.

2. Add the onion, garlic, tomatoes, butter, vinegar, molasses, chipotle puree, Worcestershire sauce, brown sugar, paprika, mustard powder, salt, and pepper to the pot.

3. Close the lid and set the cooking time to 8 minutes at high/normal pressure. It will take 7 minutes to reach pressure.

4. Allow the pressure to release from the pot naturally for 5 minutes, then quick release the remaining pressure.

5. Open the lid. Pour the sauce into a blender. Blend until smooth, being careful to hold the blender lid closed. Use immediately or store in an airtight container in the refrigerator for up to 1 week or in the freezer for up to 1 month.

Ingredient Tip

If you can't find chipotle puree, you can make your own by pureeing canned chipotle chiles in adobo sauce.

Per serving (2 tablespoons): Calories: 32; Fat: 2g; Protein: 1g; Carbohydrates: 4g; Fiber: 1g; Sugar: 2g; Sodium: 283mg

HOT PEPPER SAUCE

› MAKES 1¾ CUPS
› **Prep time:** 3 minutes
› **Pressure cook:** 2 minutes High

› **Release:** Natural
› **Total time:** 30 minutes
› 5-Ingredient

Most commercially available hot sauces contain added salt. This version is a simple whole food, plant-based recipe without any added salt, and your taste buds won't miss it. Sprinkle this sauce over anything that needs a spicy kick.

12 to 16 ounces fresh hot red chile peppers, stemmed and halved	1 cup distilled white vinegar	¼ cup apple cider vinegar	3 garlic cloves, smashed

1. Put the chile peppers, white vinegar, cider vinegar, and garlic in the inner pot and stir to combine.

2. Close the lid and set the cooking time to 2 minutes at high/normal pressure. It will take 7 minutes to reach pressure.

3. Allow the pressure to release from the pot naturally, about 15 minutes.

4. Carefully remove the lid, keeping your face away from the steam, which, depending on the spiciness of the peppers, can burn your sinuses.

5. Using an immersion blender, food processor, or blender, blend the sauce until smooth. Strain through a fine-mesh sieve and store in glass bottles or jars at room temperature for up to 6 months.

Ingredient Tip

When you make your own hot pepper sauce, you get to choose the level of spiciness. Choose hot peppers based on the amount of heat you enjoy. You can use milder green peppers such as jalapeños or serranos, a super-hot Scotch bonnet pepper, or a mix of peppers to achieve your perfect blend.

Per serving (1 teaspoon): Calories: 3; Fat: 0g; Protein: 0g; Carbohydrates: 1g; Fiber: 0g; Sugar: 0g; Sodium: 1mg

DARK CHOCOLATE SYRUP

> MAKES 2 CUPS
> **Prep time:** 3 minutes
> **Pressure cook:** 5 minutes High
> **Sauté:** 5 minutes

> **Release:** Natural for 5 minutes, then Quick Release
> **Total time:** 25 minutes
> 5-Ingredient

We love keeping a batch of this thick, rich sauce in our refrigerator for making chocolate milk or as a topping for ice cream sundaes. After pressure cooking, the sauce simmers to a satisfying syrup consistency that can be made even thicker (for a hot fudge–like consistency) with the addition of cornstarch (see the tip).

1 (13.5-ounce) can light coconut milk

¼ cup dark cocoa powder

Pinch sea salt
½ cup sugar

1½ teaspoons vanilla extract

1. Pour the coconut milk, cocoa powder, and salt into the inner pot. Whisk until the cocoa powder is well blended into the liquid.

2. Close the lid and set the cooking time to 5 minutes at high/normal pressure. It will take 7 minutes to reach pressure.

3. Allow the pressure to release from the pot naturally for 5 minutes, then quick release the remaining pressure.

4. Open the lid and select the Sauté function. Add the sugar and vanilla to the pot and simmer, stirring often, for 5 minutes or until the sugar is dissolved and the mixture has thickened. Press Cancel. The syrup will continue to thicken as it cools.

5. Store in an airtight container, such as a mason jar, in the refrigerator for 1 to 2 weeks.

Variation Tip

If you'd like your sauce thicker, remove 1 tablespoon of syrup from the pot and whisk in a small bowl with 1 tablespoon of cornstarch (for a hot fudge–like consistency) or 1½ teaspoons of cornstarch (for a thicker syrup consistency). Add the cornstarch slurry to the pot along with the sugar and vanilla extract.

Per serving (2 tablespoons): Calories: 60; Fat: 4g; Protein: 1g; Carbohydrates: 8g; Fiber: 0g; Sugar: 6g; Sodium: 12mg

QUICK HOMEMADE SALSA

> MAKES 3½ CUPS
> **Prep time:** 8 minutes
> **Sauté:** 4 minutes

> **Pressure cook:** 5 minutes High
> **Release:** Quick
> **Total time:** 25 minutes

Fresh garden salsa is made in about half the time in your Instant Pot compared to simmering it on the stove. Store this in the refrigerator to bring out when you want chips and salsa. The flavors continue to meld together as the salsa chills.

5 tomatoes, coarsely chopped

1 green bell pepper, seeded and coarsely chopped

½ onion, coarsely chopped

1 jalapeño pepper, coarsely chopped

2 garlic cloves, minced

½ cup water

½ cup fresh cilantro, coarsely chopped

1 tablespoon freshly squeezed lime juice

¾ teaspoon salt

½ teaspoon seasoning salt

½ teaspoon ground cumin

½ teaspoon freshly ground black pepper

1. Select the Sauté function. Once the pot has heated, combine the tomatoes, bell pepper, onion, and jalapeño in the pot and sauté for 3 minutes. Add the garlic and sauté for 1 more minute. Press Cancel.

2. Add the water to the pot and stir with a wooden spoon, scraping the bottom of the pot to loosen any brown bits.

3. Close the lid and set the cooking time to 5 minutes at high/normal pressure. It will take 7 minutes to reach pressure.

4. Quick release the pressure. Open the lid and remove and discard ½ cup of liquid (avoiding any chunks of vegetables).

5. Stir the cilantro, lime juice, salt, seasoning salt, cumin, and pepper into the pot. Use an immersion blender to puree the salsa. Use immediately (though let cool before serving), or store in a covered container in the refrigerator for up to 1 week.

Ingredient Tip

For a spicier salsa, double the jalapeños and add up to ½ teaspoon of cayenne pepper.

Per serving (¼ cup): Calories: 15; Fat: 0g; Protein: 1g; Carbohydrates: 3g; Fiber: 1g; Sugar: 3g; Sodium: 212mg

BACON JAM

› MAKES 2 CUPS
› **Prep time:** 5 minutes
› **Sauté:** 13 minutes

› **Pressure cook:** 7 minutes High
› **Release:** Quick
› **Total time:** 30 minutes

If you've never had bacon jam, you are missing out! This sweet and savory spread can be used on cheeseburgers, as an addition to a charcuterie spread, as an upgrade for a grilled cheese sandwich, or simply spread onto crackers.

1 pound center-cut bacon, diced	½ cup packed brown sugar	1 tablespoon Worcestershire sauce	1 tablespoon cornstarch
2 medium onions, thinly sliced	⅓ cup brewed black coffee	¼ teaspoon ground mustard	
⅓ cup water	2 tablespoons balsamic vinegar	¼ teaspoon freshly ground black pepper	

1. Select the Sauté function. Once the pot is heated, combine the bacon and onions in the inner pot. Sauté for 10 minutes, stirring often, until the onions are translucent and the bacon is almost crisp. Press Cancel.

2. Pour the water into the pot and stir, scraping the bottom of the pot with a wooden spoon to loosen any brown bits. Stir in the brown sugar, coffee, vinegar, Worcestershire sauce, mustard, and pepper.

3. Close the lid and set the cooking time to 7 minutes at high/normal pressure. It will take 5 minutes to reach pressure.

4. Quick release the pressure. Open the lid and select the Sauté function again. Remove 2 tablespoons of liquid from the pot and whisk with the cornstarch in a small bowl. Add the cornstarch slurry to the pot. Simmer for 3 minutes. While the mixture simmers, use an immersion blender to chop any larger chunks (the mixture should still be a little chunky). Press Cancel. The jam will continue to thicken as it cools.

5. Store in an airtight container, such as a mason jar, in the refrigerator for 2 to 3 weeks.

Per serving (2 tablespoons): Calories: 154; Fat: 11g; Protein: 4g; Carbohydrates: 9g; Fiber: 0g; Sugar: 8g; Sodium: 201mg

SPEEDY MARINARA SAUCE

› MAKES 6 CUPS
› **Prep time:** 5 minutes
› **Sauté:** 6 minutes

› **Pressure cook:** 5 minutes High
› **Release:** Quick
› **Total time:** 30 minutes

Because I love shortcuts and convenience ingredients on busy weeknights, I don't mind using the occasional premade pasta sauce. When I have a little more time (but not enough to slow simmer a Bolognese sauce), this versatile Instant Pot marinara is amazing with ground meat for spaghetti, for dipping bread or appetizers, for meatballs subs, chicken Parmesan, and more.

2 tablespoons olive oil

½ cup diced onion

2 teaspoons
   minced garlic

¼ cup dry red wine

1 (28-ounce) can whole
   peeled tomatoes,
   with their juices

1 (28-ounce) can diced
   tomatoes, strained
   with ½ cup of juices
   reserved

1 tablespoon
   brown sugar

1 tablespoon
   dried parsley

1½ teaspoons
   dried basil

1½ teaspoons
   dried oregano

¾ teaspoon salt

¼ teaspoon freshly
   ground black pepper

1 (6-ounce) can
   tomato paste

1. Select the Sauté function. Heat the oil in the inner pot until hot. Add the onion and sauté for 2 minutes, stirring occasionally. Add the garlic and sauté for an additional minute.

2. Add the wine to the pot and stir with a wooden spoon, scraping the bottom of the pot to loosen any brown bits. Simmer for 3 minutes. Press Cancel. Stir in the whole peeled tomatoes with their juices, the diced tomatoes with the reserved ½ cup of juices, brown sugar, parsley, basil, oregano, salt, and pepper. Place dollops of tomato paste on top, but do not stir.

3. Close the lid and set the cooking time to 5 minutes at high/normal pressure. It will take 13 minutes to reach pressure.

4. Quick release the pressure. Open the lid.

5. Use an immersion blender to puree the sauce.

6. Store in airtight containers, such as mason jars, in the refrigerator for up to 4 days, or in heavy-duty storage bags in the freezer for up to 6 months.

Ingredient Tip

This recipe is great when made with fresh herbs, as well. If you have access to them, you can use 3 tablespoons of chopped fresh parsley, and 1½ tablespoons each of chopped fresh basil and oregano.

Per serving (½ cup): Calories: 61; Fat: 3g; Protein: 2g; Carbohydrates: 9g; Fiber: 3g; Sugar: 6g; Sodium: 308mg

RASPBERRY COMPOTE

› MAKES 2 CUPS
› **Prep time:** 3 minutes
› **Pressure cook:** 1 minute High
› **Release:** Natural for 10 minutes, then Quick Release

› **Total time:** 30 minutes
› 5-Ingredient

Compote is a sauce of fruit stewed in syrup (think of a cross between jam and syrup). It can be served on desserts such as cheesecake, soufflé, and ice cream, mixed into oatmeal or yogurt, used as a pancake topping, and more. Because it is so versatile, we tend to have a jar of berry compote in the refrigerator at all times.

1 pound fresh raspberries	¼ cup sugar	2 tablespoons freshly squeezed lemon juice	½ teaspoon grated lemon zest

1. Place the raspberries in the inner pot. Sprinkle the sugar evenly over them. Let sit for 10 minutes.

2. Stir in the lemon juice and zest.

3. Close the lid and set the cooking time to 1 minute at high/normal pressure. It will take 6 minutes to reach pressure.

4. Allow the pressure to release from the pot naturally for 10 minutes, then quick release the remaining pressure.

5. Open the lid and stir the compote. Cool and serve immediately as a topping for break-fasts or desserts, or store in jars in the refrigerator for up to 2 weeks.

Variation Tip

For a delectable flavor change-up, try using orange juice and orange zest instead of lemon in this recipe.

Per serving (2 tablespoons): Calories: 27; Fat: 0g; Protein: 0g; Carbohydrates: 7g; Fiber: 2g; Sugar: 4g; Sodium: 0mg

Measurement Conversions

Volume Equivalents	U.S. Standard	U.S. Standard (ounces)	Metric (approximate)
Liquid	2 tablespoons	1 fl. oz.	30 mL
	¼ cup	2 fl. oz.	60 mL
	½ cup	4 fl. oz.	120 mL
	1 cup	8 fl. oz.	240 mL
	1½ cups	12 fl. oz.	355 mL
	2 cups or 1 pint	16 fl. oz.	475 mL
	4 cups or 1 quart	32 fl. oz.	1 L
	1 gallon	128 fl. oz.	4 L
Dry	⅛ teaspoon	—	0.5 mL
	¼ teaspoon	—	1 mL
	½ teaspoon	—	2 mL
	¾ teaspoon	—	4 mL
	1 teaspoon	—	5 mL
	1 tablespoon	—	15 mL
	¼ cup	—	59 mL
	⅓ cup	—	79 mL
	½ cup	—	118 mL
	⅔ cup	—	156 mL
	¾ cup	—	177 mL
	1 cup	—	235 mL
	2 cups or 1 pint	—	475 mL
	3 cups	—	700 mL
	4 cups or 1 quart	—	1 L
	½ gallon	—	2 L
	1 gallon	—	4 L

Oven Temperatures

Fahrenheit	Celsius (approximate)
250°F	120°C
300°F	150°C
325°F	165°C
350°F	180°C
375°F	190°C
400°F	200°C
425°F	220°C
450°F	230°C

Weight Equivalents

U.S. Standard	Metric (approximate)
½ ounce	15 g
1 ounce	30 g
2 ounces	60 g
4 ounces	115 g
8 ounces	225 g
12 ounces	340 g
16 ounces or 1 pound	455 g

Instant Pot Pressure Cooking Time Charts

The following charts provide approximate times for a variety of foods. To begin, you may want to cook for a minute or two less than the times listed; if necessary, you can always simmer foods for a few minutes to finish cooking.

Keep in mind that these times are for foods partially submerged in water (or broth) or steamed and are for the foods cooked alone. The cooking times for the same foods may vary if additional ingredients or cooking liquids are added or a different release method than the one listed here is used.

For any foods labeled with "natural" release, allow at least 15 minutes natural pressure release before quick releasing any remaining pressure.

Fish and Seafood

All times are for steamed fish and shellfish. Use the trivet to lift the fish/seafood above the cooking liquid so that it steams instead of boil.

	MINUTES UNDER PRESSURE	PRESSURE	RELEASE
CLAMS	2	High	Quick
HALIBUT, FRESH (1-INCH THICK)	3	High	Quick
LARGE SHRIMP, FROZEN	1	Low	Quick
MUSSELS	1	High	Quick
SALMON, FRESH (1-INCH THICK)	5	Low	Quick
TILAPIA OR COD, FRESH	1	Low	Quick
TILAPIA OR COD, FROZEN	3	Low	Quick

Beans and Legumes

For 1 pound or more of dried beans, use low pressure and increase the cooking time by a minute or two. Unless a shorter release time is indicated, let the beans release naturally for at least 15 minutes, after which any remaining pressure can be quick released. Beans should be soaked in salted water for 8 to 24 hours.

	LIQUID PER 1 CUP OF BEANS	MINUTES UNDER PRESSURE	PRESSURE	RELEASE
BLACK BEANS	2 cups	8 9	High Low	Natural
BLACK-EYED PEAS	2 cups	5	High	Natural for 8 minutes, then quick
BROWN LENTILS (UNSOAKED)	2¼ cups	20	High	Natural for 10 minutes, then quick
CANNELLINI BEANS	2 cups	5 7	High Low	Natural
CHICKPEAS (GARBANZO BEANS)	2 cups	4	High	Natural for 3 minutes, then quick
KIDNEY BEANS	2 cups	5 7	High Low	Natural
LIMA BEANS	2 cups	4 5	High Low	Natural for 5 minutes, then quick
PINTO BEANS	2 cups	8 10	High Low	Natural
RED LENTILS (UNSOAKED)	3 cups	10	High	Natural for 5 minutes, then quick
SOYBEANS, DRIED	2 cups	12 14	High Low	Natural
SOYBEANS, FRESH (EDAMAME, UNSOAKED)	1 cup	1	High	Quick
SPLIT PEAS (UNSOAKED)	3 cups	5 (firm peas) to 8 (soft peas)	High	Natural

Grains

Thoroughly rinse grains before cooking or add a small amount of butter or oil to the cooking liquid to prevent foaming. Unless a shorter release time is indicated, let the grains release naturally for at least 15 minutes, after which any remaining pressure can be quick released.

	LIQUID PER 1 CUP OF GRAIN	MINUTES UNDER PRESSURE	PRESSURE	RELEASE
ARBORIO RICE (FOR RISOTTO)	3–4 cups	6–8	High	Quick
BARLEY, PEARLED	2½ cups	20	High	Natural for 10 minutes, then quick
BROWN RICE, LONG GRAIN	1 cup	22	High	Natural for 10 minutes, then quick
BROWN RICE, MEDIUM GRAIN	1 cup	12	High	Natural
BUCKWHEAT	1¾ cups	2–4	High	Natural
FARRO, PEARLED	2 cups	6–8	High	Natural
FARRO, WHOLE GRAIN	3 cups	22–24	High	Natural
OATS, ROLLED	3 cups	3–4	High	Quick
OATS, STEEL CUT	3 cups	10	High	Natural for 10 minutes, then quick
QUINOA	1 cup	2	High	Natural for 12 minutes, then quick
WHEAT BERRIES	2 cups	30	High	Natural for 10 minutes, then quick
WHITE RICE, LONG GRAIN	1 cup	3	High	Natural
WILD RICE	1¼ cups	22–24	High	Natural

Meat

Except as noted, these times are for braised meats—that is, meats that are seared and then pressure cooked while partially submerged in liquid. Unless a shorter release time is indicated, let the meat release naturally for at least 15 minutes, after which any remaining pressure can be quick released.

	MINUTES UNDER PRESSURE	PRESSURE	RELEASE
BEEF, BONE-IN SHORT RIBS	40	High	Natural
BEEF, FLAT IRON STEAK, CUT INTO ½-INCH STRIPS	6	Low	Quick
BEEF, SHOULDER (CHUCK), 2-INCH CHUNKS	20	High	Natural for 10 minutes
BEEF, SHOULDER (CHUCK) ROAST (2 LB.)	35–45	High	Natural
BEEF, SIRLOIN STEAK, ½-INCH STRIPS	3	Low	Quick
LAMB, SHANKS	40	High	Natural
LAMB, SHOULDER, 2-INCH CHUNKS	35	High	Natural
PORK, BACK RIBS (STEAMED)	25	High	Quick
PORK, SHOULDER, 2-INCH CHUNKS	20	High	Quick
PORK, SHOULDER ROAST (2 LB.)	25	High	Natural
PORK, SMOKED SAUSAGE, ½-INCH SLICES	5–10	High	Quick
PORK, SPARE RIBS (STEAMED)	20	High	Quick
PORK, TENDERLOIN	4	Low	Quick

Poultry

Except as noted, these times are for braised poultry—that is, partially submerged in liquid. Unless a shorter release time is indicated, let the poultry release naturally for at least 15 minutes, after which any remaining pressure can be quick released.

	MINUTES UNDER PRESSURE	PRESSURE	RELEASE
CHICKEN BREAST, BONE-IN (STEAMED)	8	Low	Natural for 5 minutes
CHICKEN BREAST, BONELESS (STEAMED)	5	Low	Natural for 8 minutes
CHICKEN THIGH, BONE-IN	10–14	High	Natural for 10 minutes
CHICKEN THIGH, BONELESS	6–8	High	Natural for 10 minutes
CHICKEN THIGH, BONELESS, 1- TO 2-INCH PIECES	5–6	High	Quick
CHICKEN, WHOLE (SEARED ON ALL SIDES)	12–14	Low	Natural for 8 minutes
DUCK QUARTERS, BONE-IN	35	High	Quick
TURKEY BREAST, TENDERLOIN (12 OZ.) (STEAMED)	5	Low	Natural for 8 minutes
TURKEY THIGH, BONE-IN	30	High	Natural

Vegetables

The following cooking times are for steamed vegetables; if the vegetables are submerged in liquid, the times may vary. Green vegetables will be tender-crisp; root vegetables will be soft. Most vegetables require a quick release of pressure to stop the cooking process; for those that indicate a natural release, let the pressure release for at least 15 minutes, after which any remaining pressure can be quick released.

	PREP	MINUTES UNDER PRESSURE	PRESSURE	RELEASE
ACORN SQUASH	Halved	9	High	Quick
ARTICHOKES, LARGE	Whole	15	High	Quick
BEETS	Quartered if large; halved if small	9	High	Natural
BROCCOLI	Cut into florets	1	Low	Quick
BRUSSELS SPROUTS	Halved	2	High	Quick
BUTTERNUT SQUASH	Peeled, ½-inch chunks	8	High	Quick
CABBAGE	Sliced	3–4	High	Quick
CARROTS	½- to 1-inch slices	2	High	Quick
CAULIFLOWER	Whole	6	High	Quick
CAULIFLOWER	Cut into florets	1	Low	Quick
GREEN BEANS	Cut in halves or thirds	3	Low	Quick
POTATOES, LARGE RUSSET (FOR MASHING)	Quartered	8	High	Natural for 8 minutes, then quick
POTATOES, RED	Whole if less than 1½ inches across, halved if larger	4	High	Quick
SPAGHETTI SQUASH	Halved lengthwise	7	High	Quick
SWEET POTATOES	Halved lengthwise	8	High	Natural

Index

Acknowledgments

My husband, Nik. You are the great love that inspires art. Words cannot express how grateful I feel to be your partner. My kids, Grayson and Sawyer. Your creativity, energy, support, and perspective inspire me daily. Never stop being unapologetically yourselves. My mother and father, Lorraine and Ramón. Not only for teaching me how to cook, but also for your unwavering support of my dreams, no matter how big. I hope you know how much it means to me.

My dear friends, Stacey, Terri, and the TKN girls. Your love, friendship, and support have been a lifeline. The Fab Foodies community, with a special shoutout to Lindsay.

Callisto Media and Rockridge Press. I am honored that you have entrusted me to bring this second cookbook to the world.

About the Author

Ramona Cruz-Peters is the author of *Pressure Cooker Cookbook for Beginners* and the founder and Editor-in-Chief of Fab Everyday®, a lifestyle website and social media presence that reaches over 10 million people per month. Ramona currently lives in Texas with her husband, two kids, and three dogs. Through Fab Everyday, Ramona inspires people to incorporate more fabulousness in everyday life through quick recipes, easy home décor and entertaining ideas, and life hacks. Ramona's recipes and projects have been featured in *Allrecipes Magazine, Good Housekeeping, Country Living, BuzzFeed, Parade, Reader's Digest,* and more. Keep up with Ramona and all her recipes and lifestyle tips at FabEveryday.com and @fabeveryday on social media.

CPSIA information can be obtained
at www.ICGtesting.com
Printed in the USA
JSHW011024310322
24459JS00007B/37